SLIPPING THE LEASH

SLIPPING THE LEASH

**GRAHAM HARTILL
PHIL MAILLARD
CHRIS TORRANCE**

AQUIFER

Published in the United Kingdom in 2015 by

Aquifer Books
www.glasfrynproject.org.uk

ISBN: 978-0-9928438-3-0

Cover image by Phil Morsman
Cover Design by Aquifer
Photographs of the Authors: Val Maillard

CONTENTS

CHRIS TORRANCE

'Aneirin slipped the leash/to spurt through the crags of available language,/a coarse and glistening grain'

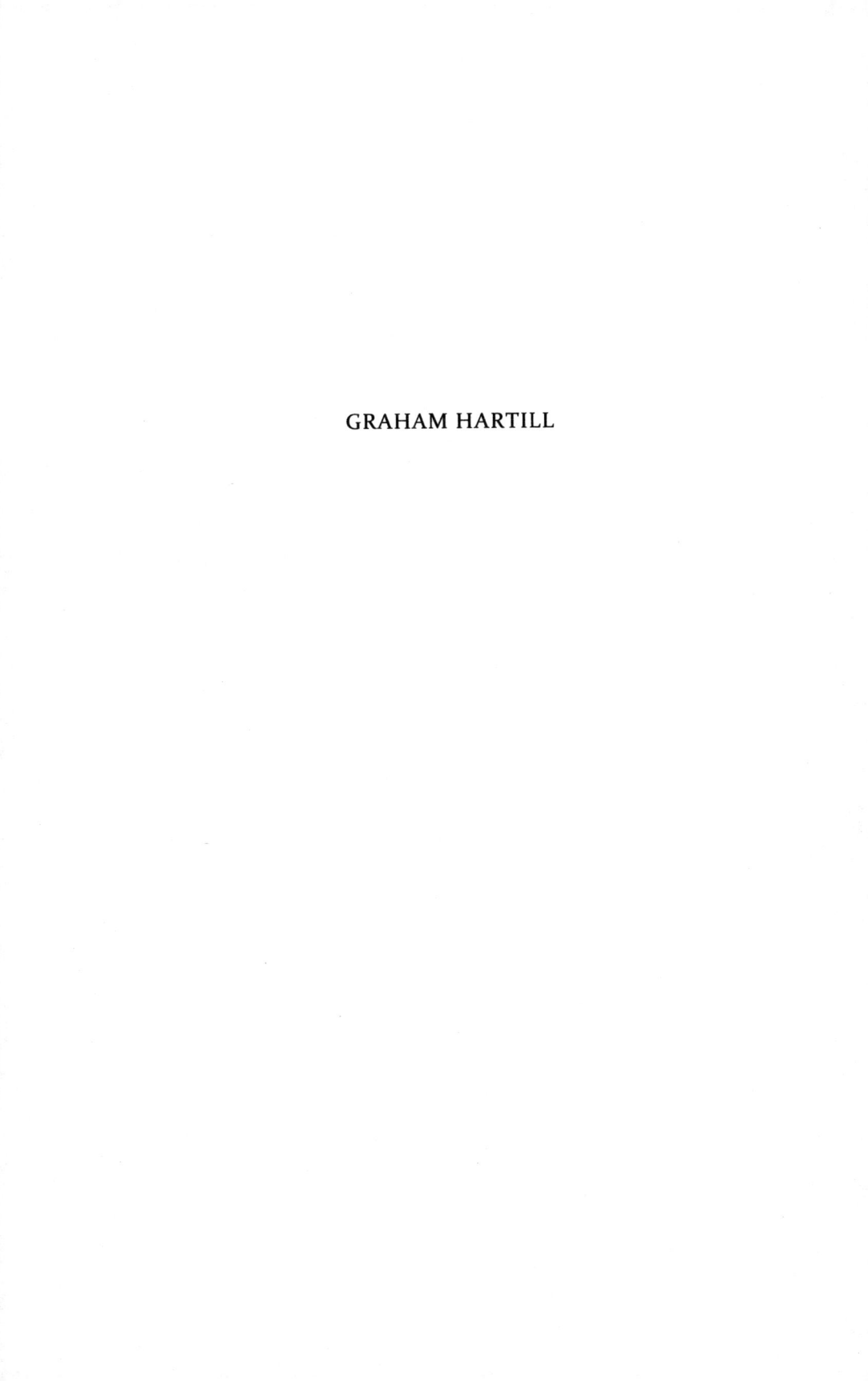

GRAHAM HARTILL

After Goddoddin (1)

Some verses grew like a tree
from a red-wet field -

its leaves flicker: "this is the Gododdin, sung by Aneirin":

the Stone-White Book of the Dead,
the Red-Green Book of the Living,
the Piss-Hide Book of War.

This is the bloody Gododdin, "sung by Aneirin".

*

Eidyn =
Edinburgh.

What was a 'city' then?
Where stood the fort of the Gododdin?
Those heroes strode was it
here?
where a squall runs past us up the old volcano's side
and a bee is hanging
soft,
black-legged,
dead, in a thorn-bush,
bright as the loch below is reflective
as any gap in a manuscript?

*

Roads like armour-straps wrap
and sparrows buckle from post to wire
shop-rooves of Catraeth, now Catterick,
sung as:

the Snow-Marble Book of the Martyrs,
the Grass-Gold Book of Survival.

Aneirin slipped the leash
to spurt through the crags of available language,
a coarse and glistening grain,
to chant the heroes,
those who with their shoulder-companions
died at Catraeth;
those feather-hearted thugs
who ravens thanked for filling their beaks
and eagles thanked,
yet are now just brooches of cloud-shadow
on a sloping field
in wolf-shape,
ox-shape,
sea-horse,
stag -

whose signatures are buried deep under stones and streets.

From Eidyn to Catraeth
the only tribute to these slain
Aneirin 's -
leaves that fall today like sun
in elegiac rain.

Remains of Issui

Tradition claims that a holy man named Issui had a cell nearby, probably in the dingle and near to the holy well still to be seen there. From his cell Issui instructed the people in the Christian Faith and won their affection. We can well imagine their distress when he was murdered by an ungrateful traveller who had received hospitality in his humble cell. Because of his reputation for sanctity and the esteem in which he was held, his cell soon became a place of pilgrimage, and the well which once nourished the saint was thought to possess healing properties. In the early 11th century a wealthy continental pilgrim was cured of his leprosy by the water in the well. In gratitude he left a hatful of gold to build a church on the hill above the well and this church was dedicated in the name of St. Issui.

from the 'The Church of Merthyr Issui at Patricio' *by Canon Arthur Reed*

My ochre is easily dug from the field,
my green from the finch's wing
when Spring is curative.

Lepers,
come.

Come everyone with rotten purse-strings

        here on the rood-loft
                vine-leaves sprout from the dragon's mouth,

        the dragon sucks
                the shoots of the vine –

and find a hatful of gold on the hilltop:
stems and shoots to boil for colour,
ink from Issui's lamp-soot.

Come
to this, the Blue Hole –

below the sky, the hill,
below the hill, his well;

the warm-honey smell
            of sawn grain,
a heron,
perched beyond his cell.

+

Says Issui
to every leper:

come,

consumptives, paymasters, singers with rotted strings,
to where the ash and the holly break
      from the dead bole of the yew

                  – the leper's body:
                        clumps of hard red wood in knee and brow,

                  spurts holly,
                              shining ash -

and ask for a fish from the heron's bill.
No traveller leaves unwashed, unfed;
one may kill, another bequeaths
a hatful of gold
            to build a church for Issui
                  up the hill.

+

Vine-leaves sprout from the dragon's mouth,
the dragon devours
            the limbs and veins of the vine.

Says Issui:

my ochre is easily dug from the field,
my green from the woodpecker's wing,
my black from lamp-soot,

come

and see.

My toes may bump the crimson bones of the twisted yew,
my hair be snagged on fence-wire,
still my fingers burn this hole in the blue;

you lepers,
pursers,
hydrophobes,
verbicides,

come and feel.

+

Says Issui,
hear:

– comes
the singer
goes –

his glee is struck from a fret of black and gold.

Cloch Cennau / Cennau's Bell

".......directing her journey beyond the Severn and there meeting with certain woody places she made her request to the Prince of that country that she might be permitted to serve God in that solitude. His answer was that he was very willing to grant her request; but that the place did so swarm with serpents that neither men nor beasts could inhabit in it. Presently prostrating herself in fervent prayers to God, she obtained of him to change all the serpents and vipers there into stones. And to this day the stones in that Region doe resemble the windings of Serpents through all the fields and villages...

Many years being spent by her in that solitary place, the holy Mayd returned to the seat of her nativity. Where, on the topp of a hillock seated at the foot of a high mountain she made a little habitation for herself; and by her prayers obtained a spring there to flow out of the earth; which by the merits of the Holy Virgin afforded health to divers infirmities..."

At Cennau's Well

What's my name?

Is it Cennau
    Keyne
        Keyne-wiri?

Whatever it was, I lost it across the estuary,
    I dropped it in that desart place the other side of the Severn,
        driving the serpents into the stones,
            deriving a kind of silent heaven

and now my name is just a place
    where jets and lorries clamber throughout my
        clouds, vibrate my bridges –

What's my name?
Is it Ceneu
    Keyna the Virgin
        Keyne?

and what's this place but a bigger body,
    a musculature of stones and beasts and jungled ridges?
        Whatever the name, I am now become this territory,
                such as -

        foxhole,
            steppingstone,
                dyke,
                    and ditch

I am become its bell, and my mouth will be buried,
    stuffed with leaf and twig, and rich with spider and silver worm

my Father-God will always burn –

I am his bell and was rung before the mechanic, the
    metalled road, I sung when even the church
        was only a glade of stubble, a slab of stone with sockets
    for oil and water, a congregation of speechless rubble

I am a daughter of red-haired Brychan,
    daughter of burning –

        before the roadmap, almost before the furrow,
            I fixed this oratory (log for lintel, twisted branch
                            for a roofridge -
                shoulder and backbone)

        the first smoke of the valley rose from my circle
                of stones

and now the fox winks at the window, an otter tumbles and
churns throughout my blood –

    I married this wood.

+

I married this wood -

     and beat my tongue in prayer like tempering bell-metal
- slow-worm soul-work - beating a blade
      to hack a path
        through plagues of brambles,
      the body's jungles.
When I was south of the Severn, "that desart place",
I cured an epidemic, freezing the snakes into ammonites -

    but now I know that the codes of the corn and
         the river will twist
     and swell for ever, things will always fall in love
with soil and water, crawl into bed with fire –

tonight, the lips of the fire and water whisper
   "Take and eat - this is my body"

but here there is no mirror
     but rain-drenched rock, no love-lamp but the
         whinchat's breast –

I am Keyna the Virgin, and whisper my vespers to crowded sky
         and wet black soil -

   I am Cennau - a river in anger,
    Keyne-wiri the buzzard,
         circling to rest

+

The Lord does use me –

I am his loophole
  foxhole
    dyke
      and ditch

    his pier
      steppingstone
        ditch
          and shield

        his scrivener
          index
            grapnel
              lifebuoy
                gin

So how can my service today be anything other than these –
each letter a scribbled sun-stitch?

Slowly as serpents, the words uncurl,
  the loin-pressure twists, unfurls
    and every phrase and cob in the drystone wall
      that stammers across the pasture
  knows that the code of the corn and the clouds, the law of
                            genetic cities,
    the clasp of the body's book,
    will be broken,

      the Word will awaken.

          +

Cennau's Medicine

China clay
      bevelled and pressed by the potter's thumb –

   the eyes are sprung!

    she leaps into the world

      +

    it is con/fusion to him who comes to be looked at –
    her eyes skewif, her ear
    tilts to an osprey's shriek
              in a distant gin

     +

   her one eye rests upon you

    leaves

     like a crow's wing

  dusting snow

    +

   she knows a man's shadow's
     a handle
    for ghosts to grip

  to lift him
    out of the world –

she feels his rocking shoulder and the sliding, agonising vein
sees each and every blink in the dazzling
Suit of Lights

+

she knows –
his need of the ball-court,
his joy and terror
to lift aloft the embroidered stave,
the gilded buckle,
the goggling head

+

and so, this girl is gagged by the witch of plague,
this tribe misplaced their king –

its ancestors are stalking through the hallways
hanging by their heels
from rain-drenched thatch

+

the badger knows his patch of earth
the otter smears his tar-marks on the guidance-stone

but we know one another,
need a ritual strong as ringing bone

+

her mind is with the grass-waves,
jumping with the river-fish

or startled, like a game-cock
shattered from grasses,
a driven pig

she charges the dirt-path's loop
towards her oratory - here the roof
is thatched with hair
and a twisted back for a ridge

+

she takes you in at face-value,
fish-bone lipped, her eye ignites
the leaves and branches of your skin –

ablaze you know the kindness of the body-bell,

its tapering ring

First Moon: at the Dragon's Head

..........*ssiang!*

daylight –

stroking the silver strings

*

listen –

mist –

sifting the stones and reflective laurel

the house a heron

rising out of the black pool

*

.....*ssiang!*

I wake again from a dream of ruins

          this house is a book -

chimney

window

roof

scalp

& eye

& tooth

*

somedays we see the herons along the river –

where do they sleep I wonder?

and how the ancestors?

*

if they're not planted fast, it's said

their hair will grow for ever

somewhere the heron lifts like light

from the black river

*

path

and wall

and crocus shoot

vein

and rib

and foot

a shovel clangs on far-off tar
a sparrow singing

      "here
      I was born"

*

the Winter dawn

stroking her silver strings

*

Note to First Moon:

"*The songs contain a number of meaningless cries or exclamations, and at the caesura of each line is the exclamation hsi which may represent the panting of the shaman in trance... One might expect the Spirit to speak through the shaman's mouth. The shaman, says a writer of the first century A.D., 'strikes the dark strings' (probably a shaman name for a kind of zithern) and brings down the dead who speak through his mouth.*"

Arthur Waley, in his introduction to *The Nine Songs: A Study of Shamanism in Ancient China.*

The New Year

The year began like a damp fox
stretching its paw from the hedge.
We slept till late, and when we rose
the valley to the south was full of mist,
the sky above the mountains yellow in the rain.
Sparrows scratched the tin on the caravan roof,
the trees stood cold and empty,
rising from their hoops.

Walking the River Wye our minds,
beside each other, drifted – when we spoke it tended to be of
the same thing at the same time.
This was the 80's, when wealth
was gathered to the businessmen, the gamblers –
                        Tao Yuan Ming
lay scorn on every aspect of government business,
tending his path and pasture, rewarding his friends for their help
with a bottle of wine.

The river was full to its banks and grey
with the strength of an army.
South, in Gloucestershire, the trains were blocked
and could not pass.
                        He wrote:
"The empty boat glides on –
whoever comes must go –
the ups and downs can never touch our freedom,"
emptying his jug of Kiangsi wine.

And drinking wine all night
they poured themselves over the ancient poems
sorting out all the differences of interpretation.

The river was glancing
through gullies and hedges,
regarding us, retreating
under an iron sky, that twisted,
turning like an ancient poem.
                        (*for Ursula*)

Silver John

"When evening shadows lengthen, it is not difficult to believe that the reedy little tarn of Llyn Hilyn, near New Radnor, is haunted by the spirit of a murdered man whose body was thrown into it.

The murdered man was known as Silver John because of the silver buttons he wore upon his coat. By some he is said to have been a cattle drover, by others a skilful bone-setter and charmer, especially expert in curing sick animals..."

A Dream Song Of Silver John

I'll crack your joints stretched backward on a hay-bale,
then kick you good up the arse.
What's up?
                        I'll yank your neck like a goose.
What ails you,
                        that a kick in the balls wouldn't cure?
Crack your arm across your back
and haul you up like a bag of grass.
I'll double you up like a mouldy carpet from out of some old
                                        woman's kitchen.

I'll pull your spine so fast and straight you'll shoot all over the straw.
You'll yelp like a cock taking fright at a fox
it'll curdle the milk in the goat
and back'll pull out straight and your knuckles go off like a gun.
I'll kick your bladder around all over the barn.
and pummel your guts like a red-faced wife at the doughboard.
I'll claw them out and wrap them round your neck and pull
                                        them tight
                        till –
I'll tear your wick off and feed it to frisky hens.
I'll tug off your toenails and use them for fishhooks.
I'll rip out your glottis and stick it in mine and sing your songs
then I'll go to your mucky house and I'll murmur your own
                                        sweet things
to your daughter and wife and son.
Your tongue'll make a supper cheap for your fat blue cat.

I'll suck out your eyes then stick them back the wrong way round,

so when I'm done you won't know whether you're coming or gone -

*

Walking

Silver John is wandering the lanes from Kington to Builth. He's covered himself with moons, which jingle between the hedges. Money moons, his pay for broken ankles, black blood, bedroom trouble. Owen pulled his shoulder out, heaving a calf from a big Welsh Black; Robson was born with a tangled leg, a spastic branch, half-ripped from his hip. Now they're slaving away in their barns again. And John has been and gone.

He pummels the living daylights out of you, stretched dreadfully over a bale. Now Silver John is treading his old familiar line, humming his circuit. He takes his time today, it's sunny, his collie scratches and twists on a yard of string. His hair is matted brown, his jacket stitched from bits of a hundred others. He smokes his scut and mutters his songs, the fluttering of throatwings fills the familiar bending hill. He treads his tunes on scabrous heel and toe.

He understands cows and dogs, and one or two women say women. At sunset, his jingling racket sets fire to polished leaves along his way. Tomorrow a pint and a flake of silver to toss you over a lump of hay and ring your ears. But now we are walking along with John to the dark, later to be so secret and bold and loud in the whispers and oily light of a high valley cowshed.

*

His Sickness

Catch your own reflection in his buttons,
his 30x30 pieces.
Silver John's no saint,
   no healer,
   poet,
   priest.

28

Is not a man.
Silver John's mother put cakes all over your body,
    then chewed them, one by one,
her sin-eating song in her nose full seemly.

He doesn't inhabit a house,
    or flat,
    or tent,
    or van.
He doesn't live nowhere.
John absorbs your illness.
You name it:
    gut-rot, mad cow, second childhood.
Viruses beg him to let them come to him.

He prays for them to infect his songs
    so that no-one can understand him.
He makes up stories about his granny's drum,
his Japanese sister,
    the moon he embraced.
His tongue is as hot as a horseradish.

No Jobseeker's Allowance,
    SS snoops,
    nor Neighbourhood Watch for John.
    No Boots the Chemist or Marks & Sparks or Currys frozen
                                    doorways.
Just an ague, and a walk, a walk, a walk.

Don't fret,
he won't tell anyone about
    your itch,
    your dizziness,
    your vacancy.
You're safe with him.

This money he wears,
    is a thousand mirrors

and after all,
   your offerings.

*

Lay hairclips then,
   and broken bits of mirror,
   corners of postcards,
   little plastic bulls,
   and smeared algae jamjars
down at his well, his watering hole.

Listen hard to the woodpecker,
learn his rattle.
And then to the tick of the wood beetle.

Welcome the moth to your thumb,
and the bat to your bedroom.

Stick your head in the fox's den
put Golden Syrup out for badgers.

Paint your breast with wasps.

Look after nature's people.

*

(*I'm hating and holding tight another wound-schism, driving along in a swirl of domestic anger, till finally a phone call finally puts the world to rights and frees me to wander on, to further dwell on those shiny coins "that were his eyes", a coat completely drenched wherein his killers saw themselves reflected, protective mirrors.*

    "The Radnor Boys pulled out his eyes..."

So why did they ring the bells? Getting shot of the scapegoat, the Judas, showing off his (no, that's our) blood-money, fear and jubilation, guilt and liberation, all drowned out in a golden, banging flood.

Scab-ridden kerb-crawler, free-loading cunt of the ditches, (might as well call them gutters), who the hell did he think he is?

Well, he's a story.

Janice, an Irish woman, rings me up to talk about her stories: "In the last few days you see I've lost my sight, it happens from time to time since I had my stroke. Well, and I can't walk or write, so my carer Mary has to do it all. I tell it all to her and she writes it down for me and types it up."

In New Radnor church it occurs to me that the darkness that smote the world when Christ died was the horror of our not being looked upon.

"I'm sorry for ringing you up so early in the morning, but I lose track of time you see."

I wonder did John fear death by water?)

*

A Second Dream Song

Oak-roots heave at the gale-clouds
the sky is green and waving, full of fruit

Every babe is born with Deuteronomy on his buds
the sea is solid salt, as bare as brass

Every day a man goes fishing in his attic
helicopters flap about like gold-red fish in pools

Sailors, when they're hungry, far from home, eat fog
The King, that spider in a crown, craps oats

The sea pulls back, reveals the altar of the world –
inverted oak, its root-claws yank at gales

*

*Ending up at the 'reedy tarn' Llyn Hillin, where John was
drowned, to observe the molten, softly swaying, lemony green of
the reeds and the splash and the dip and the cruise of the coots.
Despite the cutting through of regular day-out traffic to Builth
and the barbed wire fence, it's beautiful, shining blue in warm
summer light, against the benevolent slopes of today's story.*

*The blue, the green, the fawn and the steel of the fence and the
red of the Citroen parked on the gravel, resolve themselves to the
white of the only outcome that doesn't deny a thing.*

*"...Some doggerel lines dating from about the time of the murder
commemorate the crime, and in days gone by, it was asking for trouble
to recite them within the hearing of a New Radnor man. The verse ran:*

> *Silver John is dead and gone*
> *So they came home a-singing;*
> *The Radnor boys pulled out his eyes,*
> *And set the bells a'ringing."*

(Eric L. King)

*

Walking Towards His Death

Tonight my body's a tower of silence.
I'll die next Tuesday at half-past ten
not from cyanide or powdered granite
but tossed in a pond like a shit-tailed kitten,
an insignificant village.

Out beyond the coast there was a country,
ancient roads lead nowhere to it.
A thousand died at Cantre'r Gwaelod,
the night Seithenyn, the floodgate guard,

got smashed on apple wine.
    Now axe-welts shimmer in lapping water,
clumps of hawthorn, willow, fir.
And teacups drip from fishermen's hooks.

Out beyond the coast of what we know,
there's still a body, places that recur.
Tuesday, I'll gulp down
pulverised diamonds,
and leap at the edge of your mind for good
a slapping silver fish.

Winged Heads

*The chief outlet for popular art in Wales has always been the
tombstone. In the days when popular religion, popular art and
popular emotion were all one and the same thing, it was very
often fine. The most famous Welsh lapidarists were the Brute
dynasty, whose work you may find in many churches and
graveyards of Gwent and Powys.*

- Jan Morris

*...chubby cheeked cherubs, not very dire angels...executed with
unabashed primitivism...*

- Richard Haslam

*(tossed on the Grwynefechan stream to honour the sons of Brute
who lived here: Thomas, Aaron, John, from 1698-1834)*

a voice of all 3:

Dip, then drench
your brush-tip

– bluebell,
cherry,
violet –

warm Patricio's sill
in heavy drifts
of sun –

and stroke an angel's grin from it.

And try (in vain!)
to space
your lettering

                with grace!

    – it is a life's farewell.

                    *

The human face pokes out from oak or stone;
bark and cloud are figured as ourselves.
Reflect your order in their formlessness,
        (as I can call you *You*
    eh light?)

as something bubbles up in shape of happiness,
        (it might as well be Redon's, or Traherne's,
    who *dove* in colour!)

We're a common man,
an artist too,
for art *is* common;

sons who delved in summer
        (wall of forest with the wind in it,
    a capsized sky),

who saw each head as bud
sprung out of every second
of shit meets seed.

We're Imager,
who know you have to crook the eyes
for lifelikeness,
whose old cracked house, we know
will drift and change
        (fires and plastic added,
    damp, for now! rerouted).

And, like a house requires a roof
to call it *house*,

we also needs a finish –

*

For what is left throughout the sifting body
let alone from body unto body,
death to life?

Our secret recipe for dye
was written on the fly-leaf of a Bible
so it's said,
and burnt
inside this house –

   but now we're truly dead
and are not telling!

So let the secret
be just that;
your mind make pattern
out of what is drenched,
and what is not.

*

Somewhere in the past there is a family
   ill-lit;
a ghost is standing in the river –

give her dark red pears
and grass-feathers.

We're a common man,
like best the newness of the day
   my God –

*

Resign your breath –
for when the human compost kisses seed
there is an eloquence of lilac, gold!

*

Like coalsmoke breasts the roof-air
try to cut your script not stiff nor crippled,
    lax nor illegible.

*

Fill your baby's cheeks with damsons
and his hair with butter!

*

Here is neither certainty nor accident,
yet brims with wasp and oak!

*

And, like the surgeon or the shoemaker,
we keep the right as artist
to append our signature!

(for Liz Pitman)

Fishkey

1

Jackdaws tousle blue in this,
the year's first sun to speak of;
a shitten sheep departs a lamb in a cracking orchard,
white-bloody branch-meat tousled on shiny tar.

This winter's murrain buckled the cattles' backs –
   their only cure a cupful of crystal,
     filched from a font;
       and God,
   your face is pinked by the centuries,
     eroded, nobodied,
   crouched in your studded *du'at*.
   the 4 Evangelists fingering the lozenge,
     elverine, swinging through murk.

            *

  At Peter church
imagine his anxious neck
shuddering up the rutted, leaf-shuttered lane
3000 miles from Rome, in flight from the sable and pearl
   to avalanche-belted outposts:
oaksmoke sharp in Silurian thickets,
dog-rave, flanking the blankness –
then, at last! the kneesore grace of farmcradles, moss-headed barns;
   the locals gawp, and are rocked at the sight of him –

   And *these* the Gates of Heaven?

            *

  He flipped a trout in a well
and fingered a key to the gleam of mythic geography,
   made yellow splash of sun –

   this story is the day!

2

Have trust
the day will come
when ragged, dishonoured language
will be recognised.

This is it:
the ordinary ridges, flushed with praise
and deafness.

I'm come to think of them
collected, gifted,
out beyond my life.

Cwmyoy, July

It's nothing new
to realize this Christ,
emaciated, slipshod,
dislocated
as this church risks dislocation, demolition, by geology,
yet hangs together, crooked,
   human:
square-jawed, wide-browed,
recognisable head,
arms stretched straight
as if those starving ribs need *us*,
our modern skin
(well-fatted from an acreage so good
and yet our local foot-and-mouth-fucked farmers say
it's barely worth an economic toss);
who wants us as a man would
who's become unsure (his cross)
that wisdom really does mean giving up
all future,
but holding together enough
to stay
a place to come to,
buckled like the body bucks
with age
and every increment of knowledge.

Bhopal

(On the 20th anniversary of the disaster)

A bluetit flashes to a twig.
It's raining; there's plenty
of bluetits in God's green country,
you could drink the rain
and the quinces are yellow,
yellow, my favourite colour.

In every word like *yellow* there lives a space
that nature's imagination fills with a thousand others;
this space is where we stand or fall.
The wars that are big and the wars that are small
are really the same imperative:
cash, that keeps our death abroad.
But Breughel's hellish torches scorch us everywhere,
and the searing gap between each one of us
is once what God but now international finance rushes to fill.
Our horror is not to be found as hell elsewhere
but methyl isocyanite seeping up through the world's skin.

*

Good clean water from 60 feet below reliable clay and granite:
this is what we've got in Wales, thank God.
"For us it is not an important failure":
one by one we carry on towards some place we think we've got
to get to.

This is how you make a poem at a distance:
but hell is not imaginary
nor theological;
nor is bliss: clean water, bluetits.
Welcome to the world.

Brochwell Looks Back On Melangell

I felt like a bird that stooped to the hare in me.
All my life I'd been told to trample the womanly thing,
our game being power and heavy skill,
but when I fell, my sins
flew off from me like flies from cess
and I didn't know where to put my eyes,
that little animal trembling under her skirt!
She looked like a hedgehog, an urchin run off from an orphanage,
some baggage on the loose, with hair hung down like scruffy willow.
   "So what do you *really* want to see?" she said.
I spat and tossed my hat off, but she didn't move
(the little animal bucking beneath her skirt).
Her eyes were waving grey and black, like poplar trees in wind
and I was pinned by them, thrown back against my scorn.
Oh yes, she knew I could have captured more than just a hare!
But I just stood.

   And that's what got to me: a falcon
tumbling to a prey I suddenly didn't recognise,
   I sheered off.

That hare was like a little Christ sent skipping to his mother's thighs.

                     *

   Look, I must do something more
than merely tell you this. The words
are just too plain, not plain enough.

   You poets know it:
words are little gods to you.

   I've tried to hunt the word with enough of God in it
      to do her right.

   And when I'm dead, please pin a little scratch of skin of me to
                              Peter's door –

42

it seems like all my life's been battering it.

*

Since Melangell
I've set the dogs on men
and forced a girl or two, like soldiers do
    (Well poets, what do you expect?)
But lying down with her would be a softer, sadder thing:

  her skull so velvety and scarred,

    her breast a tent for all my violent griefs,

      my sins descending on us through the night
      like bright and ceaseless rain.

A Chase

"Behold upon Walter Brut,
Whom bisiliche thei persue den,
for he said hem the soothe..."

    – Piers Plowman

         – and they set the glass-toothed dogs on him
by whispering from the King, and one-by-one
their jeeps pulled out of driveways, thudded onto tracks;
hunt-followers, tightarse-piled on donkeys,
cluttered through the sagging bridles, in and out of thorn-grasps,
sweating fog –

         but he was hid in some undazzled house,
the fatwa baffled by a net of news: a worm
strung soft between homesteads.
Rat-lofts, plum barrels, hay:
               his diving-holes.

    Was it he or was it the forest riding?

Between the domes and buttes he fluttered, from darren to graig,
the soft blue skin of his oxford-pummiced fetlocks skinned, his roan
                       addled.
He tottered to a canyon black and briar-boarded, thicked, uncastled,
bracketed with dippers, brigands, swine,
occult with bramble-twine and knobbled crosses:
pillow of black-mailed thigh and throstle-eggs for breakfast,
a poke-faced grave of sherrifs.

        And, like *Troed Troeth*, the hog,

    his numbered bones, his saturated forelock, flora
caparisoned, the trophies of the woods upon him

      hot-pursued,

by brass-indignant spurs and glossy pork-fat necks
that jostled for halloo of him to trumpet to the King.
    But Walt was gone –

                    from the flourishing gaze of the retinue,
from crystal celebrity, infamy,

              gone –

from the clutch of the claw-brained councils,

                    gone –

to a badger sett for giants:

          Grwynefechan

there he stuck –

   his head in a sack,

   his head in a boat of straw,

   to spend New Year.

       *

Star-pinched:
   a tattered gutter,
a solo carp in a pond.

       *

   and the occasional rattle of oaths,

receding

Sanctuary

(to Llanthony)

Or: he came to a place of sheer mental rock
that cannot give, that is eternal
in its suffering: banal, entangled, terrified,
that he'd been knowing
for a thousand years –
                              before he was even born
his life was as impassable as this.

   The hunt was on, but such is the way of things
each moment forgot the last. He headed off
again and again, for meat and sport.
But then, in his middle age
he found he was stranded, ransomed
by a landscape thick with thieves, and fallen trees,
his body hunting him.

A luminous stag, a cross between its horns
so tenderly gripped, was given to his mind.
A lucky break.
                    We see the rest of the story
"even today" in the tower that he hammered
to the World: that time means less than nothing
to the ravens.

                    Still,
this is the kind of place necessity still brings you to,
though matters of the heart drive on

From Crug Hywel

(Abiezer Coppe interrogates the ghost of Hywel Dda, "the Law Giver")

Hywel Dda,
"the Great",
I call you out –
    from the wind-burnt ridge beyond *Pen Cerrig Calch*.

Hywel Dda,
"the Good", these rocks are arctic white.

          *

The sun this winter afternoon is splintered in my eye,
    your name is splintered –

    Are you Offa, cementing his wall with blood?

        Or Qin Shih Huang De, who built the greatest of all walls,
        and in which building, hundreds of thousands were buried?

    Are you Hywel the Good, the Protector, the Law Giver?

    Or Shadow-Hywel?

Answer.

    It's said you had a man at supper, under the table, to scratch your
                                      foot

    another solely "to seek the burden of straw for the prince's bed".

And answer this –

    you are one thousand years dead.

          *

I've practised a word or two,
tempered a sword
to rattle the rocks and the grasses,
to thrash at the thorns of your rhetoric,
to hack at the clasp of your body's book –

Are you the King of the Craven Bay,
whose throne is a Bute Town high-rise
and whose banners are the tattered plastic bags that drape the
                    trees of Taff around Llandaff Cathedral,
whose Sacred Way is the ringroad, stilted, swerving past the
                    ruined pub and the Kim Wah Sung,
whose braziers burn with the stink of tyres, bonfires back of the
                    Beldam Rubber warehouse?
Does your army ebb and flow in liquid crystal digits, poisoning
                    work in its sleep,
whose field of triumph is the carpark back of Asda?
Is your bloodline the milky ditch behind the Rover Way
                    industrial estate,
whose tithe is negative equity,
whose herds are smiling faces smeared on billboards,
            white on white on white?

Hywel,
I want to forget your name,
I want to see your face.

I'll give you a thousand names,
names as blue as jayfeathers.
I'll call you out

from the scatter of arctic rocks on a sunburnt ridge,
from an innocent saucer of stones,

to dress you in the rags of gulls,
a blackthorn tree in flower

and summon you into time.

I'll give you over a thousand names,
a name for every year of your age.

I'll call you out of *me*,
my fist and foot,
for all identity's mistaken
and writing is the "memory of the tribe",
eroding as the hills erode.

Your fort wears down,

   its mud-blonde paths are crumbling,

for this is the love of earth.

       *

We talk and walk the ditches –
a flash and then the afterburner growl
a second from Brecon,
tail-lights winking, devouring speech.

A country is a vortex in the global speculative flow,
                a customer.
But an expression doesn't only speak about someone
but asks ourselves to speak,
and is true commerce,
face-to-face relationship
with that which is.

The possibilities of tyranny are endless,
with unlimited resources:
hunger and beneficence,

love, and wealth
and their withholding,
silence and rhetoric –

but he that expresses himself,
that *faces* me,
says no to me
or yes to me,
opposes any power that I seek,
gives me his absolute No
to any possibility of killing him,
his freedom.

And war becomes suicide,
death by mistaken identity.

                    *

Deliver us
Hywel, Son of Cadel,
pen a moliant yr holl Frytaniad –
the Head and the Glory of All the Britons!
My lips are juiced by Taliesin's berries,
we walk the jewel-mouthed circle of his mountain retinue.

They ask me –
is there an infected cow's tongue flapping in my chest?
Am I a moth,
a stuttering pebble?

Speech erodes
and this is the love of earth.
And if we will weigh one another
let us be weighed as the feather is weighed
(as a handful of jayfeathers, shining blue in a red clay jug on a
                    kitchen sill in rainy slanting light)

            – let us be weighed with care

            *

Your eyes are the pools that swell in fields
when the wind is weeping!

Our cities will become the rags of thrush and buzzard.

Your crotch a blackthorn tree.

A Sky-Blue Book of Taliesin:

Taliesin's Thanks To Elphin

With me you resurrect the knowledge
of the 150 ciphers:
which tree is king of what we are to everyone,
and who caresses who in their imagination
(have no fear, *everybody* does it!);
this, all this
for saying Hello to a rising moon from out of a mental estuary,
white as a piglet.

Thank you for keeping an eye out,
for passing by
and watching the shudder of lines that glint and infinitely break
,
and hooking me back
to the painful light
of something to mean –

to this I will free you too.

                    *

Gwion To You

What would I be if I wound up in *your* dream?
Laved with grit in a summer field,
a scarecrow in the hot pink dawn of poetry?

And what adventures would we have, together?

I'm not presuming this has any kind of meaning
    other than a poem's shape,
or expect any answer at all from the you you know.

Shields

I picked it from the field,
was given it by the field
of battle,
its patterns cut by a crippled god with blacksmith's muscles, the
                                        eyes of a jeweller,
picturing everything:
harvests, floods and marriages

only a man-god could think of a man
   like a palisade of alder,
      whose spear was sparkling wine in a vessel of glass
   for the hills, for the horse-hoards, the bee-bright mead –

this life not even Taliesin
can describe:

to try
is to make another kind
of life.

So, I give this shield to you
who are, no doubt, familiar,
having lived,
with everything that songs must be.

            *

Silver John Come Back

   "I come awake and again every road leads to a house"
                  - Ma Jian

I'll tell you what I saw
on the streets of the drowned:
bells that quietly rocked where speech should be

I've seen the soulful life
reconstituted: reek
of rotten trees, the X-ray glints
of boats -

this is the only light
I am allowed some nights.
But I get up and curse:
It Shall Be More,

progress
to live the day
through motion and the blessed dry air.
I'll tell you what I write:
There Is No Only Light.

Penrhys First Take

before the festival

People don't hold back
you feel you could walk right into their living rooms
and they'll give you a cup of tea and ask how far you've come

a pilgrim's way, the way it should be, Phil says
the backs of houses, gardens sloping full of stuff
and Rottweiler lurching over the breeze blocks just behind your neck
a burnt out electric-box, bedsteads, the usual squashed and
                                        burnt-out stuff in gardens
duck-egg, crimson peeling doors
the angular blade of the roof edges neatly, regularly, jagging the sky
pale blue and pink flowers arranged in windows perfectly
a vase of lilies in each of five
a scarlet rose in the glasswork over the perfectly painted door
ladies and schoolkids in garages all too keen to help to show you
                                        on your way

the Virgin Mary rises out of a sea of free-floating indicators
a crushed and rusted typewriter by the municipal boulders that
                                        block the path
                    to travellers, night safarists
twisted old typewriter bent into

                    T P   +

        W E   U

A   F   I
                                    K
                D
        Z X   CV

!
the Twisted Letters Of Our Lady of Penrhys
that took wing one night and flew from the back of the trashed Fiesta
the Smashed Apotheosis Of The Keyboard of Our Lady
                                    – awe fuik!

cold and wet for the time of year but then it always is these summers
two or three people waiting at the bus stop next to the virgin statue
                                                            white
pray can you do anything about our earth My Lady?

"Little Church" white painted over the doorway
lissom water with Coke bottle, crisp bag
they dragged the statue all the way to London,
burnt it there
the way they dragged a criminal or a dissenter, to his fate
a spirit of carnival, of righteousness

a revolution is the toppling of statues
seizing the totem, dragging its way to the centre of new power
leaving a gap, a heart-hole where it was before
a bereavement, a terror
because it might be you they drag away next
so you hide in a hole and you starve

we're told to make the poetry accessible
but what the hell does that mean?
well I think I know, we all know in one way
- easy to understand

What's easy to understand?

The day, this day is

Flowers

A woman met another woman
in the churchyard

she was scattering flowers
in not one spot,
all over the place

they buried her
I don't know where
my grandmother,
my workhouse
grandmother

without a place of her own

she is hungry for flowers

*

Her ghost is peering through
the window of my life

they all wore badges of course
the unmarried mothers,
the indigent of Crickhowell,
Llangattock,
Blaenavon

the workhouse was self-contained
a kitchen garden,
woods and a well

to meet its needs,
window sills
too high to see over,
sloping,
so you couldn't put anything on them

because they weren't supposed
to have a thing
anyway

because they were
no-one

*

I don't know where they put her
and so I am scattering flowers,
the poem is spring here

the flowers release her
from what we think

from being unthought about

Neo-romantic

Blaen Yr Henbant

A grey cat gnawing threads of blue rubber mouse insides
                              in sunshine on the grass –
we need to tell at least both good and ill
or no compassion's possible

at Skirrid Inn they hanged a hundred men at the foot of the stairs
but now the frogspawn's springing back
and sun's in the lanes

to be alive, and pleasant with friends
in the 21st century,

to stride past Grundy's rundown farm at the turn of the cwm:
feedbags, plastic tubing, turnips, dirty windows full of bags
                              and tins
and somewhere there's an ancient mother in there I'm told
birch-branches, mud, all over the lane

I followed a hare, dead slow, for a half-a-mile,
and then he took straight off from standing,
                              five feet leap in a hedge

I imagine Edward Thomas's tobacco scroll reminds him of a
caterpillar, propping his stick by the gate
                              a hundred years ago:
What? These ordinary things I see for you, he says, these
                              words I say for you
keeping my eye on the snow-gullies dripping down in
                    keenest light on great Crug Mawr, north,
while south the lanes are filling up with birdsong

Old blue barbs in a blackthorn bush: how brittle nature
scoffs at all our futile clutches
on this hillside acreage

he smiles at the sight of an orange, black-bushed fox
who, startled, bounces away downhill from a ruined cottage

*

How come we all don't know the hunger for beauty
all the time?
The starving for beauty
that rises inside
wide-eyed
at the light at the thought of an image,
a stupendous jewel –

and towers of music of thought in a phrase,
the massive truth
seen dazzling
in its simple complex
for the first time –

this is what we work for
some days –
all that hard work –
then the moment pops
like an astonished diamond fish

that ordinary longed-for time,
the endless
piled up on my table,
the shelves
getting wider

it comes in the shape of music,
the beautiful –
once in, you see
how blinded we are to it all,
scratching around for the grains of day-to-day
obsessed with ending as some mistake
instead of the edge that gives life shape
and is crammed with the beauty of
a jewelled music tower

*

The Green Road

The forestry is forgotten,
no, forgetting

the forest lightless,
heavy with snow,
the path through the fence
and into the forestry –
you didn't go in,
it was like a dream
of inability to move

in Summer,
the voice of Nature
rubbing the leaves –
the forgotten,
and the unforgotten

recall past recalling:
Then / The lovers came out of the wood again

the lost green road
into the heart
of Coed Ddu

(Edward Thomas: *As the Team's Head-Brass*)

Little Haven

Opening this notebook, old stuff
towards poems
that may or may not have made it:
 the year's provided the finity of it
 the infinity of it
  the making finite of it,
   & that's how the threads appear
now the threads appear again
 in this,
from an orange week
 or a pink week

You gave us such divine materials
I wrote last year, with you, the World, in mind
and now you are sour with us,
 your lovers,
 because we abuse you with –
(I'm changing it now to –)
with our good intent
to try to lead a happy life
(I had plastic & petrol)
who gave me in return
those flashing marigolds in Chris's garden
or the rainbow over Slieve Leige cliffs in 1976,
or the lobster-pink spires of Bryce

now I've opened this notebook again
with the aim of a small redemption
in the pages of the new days

*

Ursula wonders why
the mariner killed the albatross –
no reason –
except to transgress

against nature

the moral order

and this brings death and,
more problematically,

life-in-death

there is no reason,
except, as they say,

it's what we tend to do

*

Where does the poem end?
Where are its outsides
in terms of the fields
that stutter away to the silent swollen river
bouncing along with its human trophies:
furniture, cars and mirrors?

About the way we've lived till now
and can't go on living:
plastic bags stuck high in trees
(there's never one biodegraded since the first was made):

does it end in the body of the woman
sitting next to me
as our train shoots on across the lake?

*

The Great Wave
  (after Hokusai)

a late afternoon
like any other idea –
desperately trying for harbour
in the claws of the commonplace storm

way off, is the central mountain
steadfast,
imminent,

I – Not – I

Notes

Winged Heads: three sons of the Brute Family were responsible for charming and distinguished memorial slabs found in many churches around the area of their home, Glan Yr Afon, in the Grwynefechan valley of the Black Mountains in mid-Wales where this poem was written.

Fishkey: drawn on legends associating St. Peter with this area.
du'at: Egyptian gateway to the "unknown region between sunset and dawn." (Ian MacDonald)

Bhopal: the quotation is from W.H.Auden's poem *Musée des Beaux Arts* where he reflects on Breughel's painting *Landscape with the Fall of Icarus*. On December 3 1984, 8000 people died, since which the city has experienced a continuing epidemic of cancers and deformity. The Dow Chemical Company refused to accept culpability or even to clean up the deadly-toxic remains of the factory.

Melangell: "The legend of Melangell derives from two 17th century transcripts of a lost medieval Life Of The Saints. One day a prince called Brochwell was hunting at a place called Pennant. His hounds raised a hare that took refuge in a thicket. On pursuit, the prince found a virgin praying, with the hare hiding under the folds of her garment. The hounds were urged on but fled howling; the huntsman raised his horn to his lips and was unable to remove it... So impressed was the prince by Melangell's godliness that he granted the valley to her and here she founded a religious community."
 – from the guidebook to the church at Pennant Melangell.

A Chase: incorporates lines from David Jones' poem The Hunt.
Walter Brute: "Undoubtedly the most famous of

the Brute family was Walter, born in the 12th century and became notorious in his religious beliefs and expressions. He anticipated some of the beliefs of the Quakers, and held that oaths, wars and tithes were unlawful. He was a zealous advocate of religious equality and political freedom and of everyone's right to his own religious opinion. Having refused to become a clergyman, he took to farming and became known as the 'Apostle of the Black Mountains'. The bishops, priests, monks and gentry of Brecon and Hereford combined to hunt him down, and it is said that Richard II interested himself in this hunt, but through the kindly offices of the common people, the mountains, caves and forests, he escaped capture for a considerable time. A certain window at Old Castle Farm is showed to visitors as the one through which Walter Brut narrowly escaped his pursuers, departing thence to Capel-y-ffin, and eventually making his home at Grwynefechan. But in 1391 he was caught. What became of Walter Brut after this is not known."

     – from A History of Llanbedr Ystradw, by Ivor Brute

From Crug Hywel: the hill fort near Crickhowell in southern Powys, reputed seat of Hywel Dda, the ruler who unified Wales.

     Abiezer Coppe: the ranter whose work, *A Fiery Flying Rolle*, was published in 1649.

PHIL MAILLARD

NEW DECADE SONG (1980)

Name/a thing/& you gain a measure/of power
Chris Torrance, CITRINAS

In the north

        some slight earth tremors

& here in Wales

        a night full of rushing water

We go out in the tongue

        of clear Polar air

after the storm

        The steep streaming roads

are deep in lines of mud & stones

& black leaf-mulch

        White hills

ride the distance

        Up around the Forestry

we cross battlefields of smashed trees

where they have been cutting

        In the plantations

between the crowded pines

        it is gloomy

& lifeless

       To name

            is not just to gain power

but to set ourselves

           within some pattern

some pulse

        some shock wave

as the first drops of more rain

              prick the puddles

as I align a stone on the Roman road

               down a firebreak

& straight to the lights

          on the long low shed

of the open-cast at Rhigos

           bright

below the dark sweep of the ridge

NIGHT JOURNAL/SPRING DEPRESSION

INSOMNIA

A pleasure
                anticipated,
a joy
        that failed, confirmed
the truth of the lie
        of hopelessness –

                sleek cars, false blood,
                        power dreams, teratogenic movies
                        of a blank new decade –

leaving us only to lie
abed
        with cigarettes, a book, a tape
of something miserable
to cheer us, some sad thing to
enter empty, naked,
the wood
        plucked with an eagle's quill

Sadness.
Is that true?
Have I the energy
        to get this down,
                catch it all
                        flying by?
                beyond self-consciousness,
        beyond the white glare
                of the page
                        daunting

What are these thoughts,
                        these feelings?

The music ends,
I turn back
on my back,
the motion waking
whole new worlds –

the spring evening
        moon behind curtain

My energy, endogenous, cannot keep up,
        flagging with the quickening pulse,
            the lengthening light

the limp new fingers
        hung out by the horse chestnut

Yet one perfection tonight
        walking home up the hill
planet bright in fading blue
    - strong tree black - a woman,
            washing down the steps of her house
at that time of night?
            Smell of carbolic

The smell of wallflowers & exhaust fumes
        coming in the window

The tumbledown town -
        no, cut that, not
            the tumbledown town

& these words recently read -

It is an impossible conflict, naturally, but we
hold, & hold it, or fail as poets

But this dilemma,
impasse - it's what I wanted
wasn't it?
All those years ago
throwing it all away
I chose it, created it
though ignorant of it
- that how we live
is important, that's
the all of it -

The poem
no mirror
but the experience itself

reading what's written

– the all of it
that I'm trying to explain, get across
        so awkwardly,
losing it, finding it

how we live

HILL COUNTRY CONTRASTS

We walk down to the river
thinking of the old man –

    We don't know enough, he had said,
    implying no lack of detail
    no lack of information
    but a completion
               by death.

    We had sat in the parlour
    aware of time
               Time passing
    Time passing slowly
                 Tick
                    Tick of
    the old clock in the corner.

    He'd said goodbye in the garden,
    under his copper beech
    in his Sunday suit, with a box rule
    sticking out the top pocket...

We walk down to the river
through the bluebells and orchids –
3 dippers whip downstream –
you bathe, lovely mammal,
dark hair floating, miming
your tingle and chill in water
    cold from underground.

AUTUMN SONG

DARKNESS & LIGHT

Out on the moor
    in the rain
the heather is dark
    & the rushes hold the light
into themselves
    The river turns wild
foam-brown, full, fierce

    To re-enact
        my father's woe

    Dogs barking
        at either hand

    The corrupt lower Neath
    sliding slow & muddy
    through the ruins of industry
    between damp, dutiful towns,
    black wharves & breakers' yards

    The upper Neath, innocent
    with a secret knowledge
    of innocence, a leaf, dropping
    onto the pulsing surface
    of the water

A man on a bicycle
leading a horse
through the village
at dusk – sparks
striking off the road

THE 'CHICAGO IMAGISTS' EXHIBITION IN SWANSEA, JULY/AUG. '81,
AND WHAT THE CITY COUNCIL THOUGHT ABOUT IT

Tubular speech bubbles shout NO!
We have a duty to the citizens of Swansea
The shadow of a cowboy
or is it a homburg?
pleats itself across the steps
The criterion is whether members
would hang such paintings over their mantelpieces
Extraterrestrial mosaics
Encounters in a green sandstorm
A number of artists have complained
that the works aren't what they'd call good
Those sachet clouds make a BIG SKY
Fingers form the valley sides
There are schools in Swansea
with children who could paint better pictures than these
MIDNIGHT TREMOR unhinges the tower block
Inhabitants hurled into blackness
We are going down the wrong road
It's a slippery road
So those tribes are playing an electronic game
CARD BROAD pinned to the prance of death
Can anyone say they have been educated?
Sugar skulls   RED FACE
Orange peel skin   Temple teeth
grinning   Tender tattooed tart ELCINA
looks quite happy about it all
Or had their minds stimulated?
Empty eyes traced in light
We have been conned by the people we trust
All hung on the worst available wallpaper
But the Council would be made to look a laughing stock
if it withdrew the pictures now
Tiny figures in attitudes of surprise
continue the Winter-Count
on curtains, wrapping paper & lampshades

If the signature on these paintings had been Michelangelo
we would have called them classics
Cock-heads & cunt-mouths in THE BROTHEL
The Council accepted it could do nothing
But let's make sure we don't get caught
with our pants down in the future

RHYS DAVIES, RETIRING FROM GLYNMERCHER FARM

Spindly, late, rough-country primroses
out of sheep-reach
on the dripping, mossy bank

Split rock grabbed
by dead tree roots

Garlic at floor-level,
water separating from mud
underfoot
         The river
  below

Rhys Davies, leaving!
No son to farm
his father's land

No more, the visitations,
no more, the pounding of the path,
the hammer blows to the cottage door,
the dog left in the porch,
awkward silences as he sits,
cap & stick & boots

No more, the sudden pronouncements:

I don't want to be carried from here –
I want to be buried over there
- meaning Llandovery, where he has relatives
& where he has bought a smallholding

Mrs Thatcher, she's a good woman.
A strong woman.
Well, we can't all think the same,
    can we, Rhys?
Why not?
  (Slight smile)

Aye, the years are rolling by
And it's raining again.

Well, that's how it is in Wales –
2 showers a year
six months each

Well, goodbye to you.
So long as we all have good health,
that's the main thing.
Goodbye.

OLD MAN IN THE BUS STATION

Old man in the bus station

each morning – keeps himself

separate – a short plump man

with a beard, with a look

on his face – A calm look?

A blank look? A kind of

confident indifference

crossed with innocence –

Unassuming? Resigned? Amused?

None of these are quite right.

The sort of person

who would whistle softly to himself

but he doesn't.

The sort of person

who appears aimless

but in fact gets on the bus in the end

like everyone else –

but unrushed.

He's usually done up

in an overcoat, but last Thursday morning

it was so warm that even he

was wearing just a jumper

& on the jumper was a large yellow badge

& on the large yellow badge

it said

I AM AN ENEMY OF THE STATE

SEA LOCK

Summer is communion
yet anger rises

in the inner edges
of cities

where my dreams & my horror
collide

slowly
slowly in

flourishing scrub-ends
mudflats & warehouses &

undischarged emotions
anger rising

in ragged fever
a morning haze

where we pick early blackberries
through wire

in shade of
rusting wheels

where a whole technology
ran out of steam

in lush wasteground
anger rises

AN AFTERNOON AND EVENING WITH JOHN TRIPP
who died in February 1986

From the train the fields are frosty in hedge-shadow
and flood-ponds lightly frozen.
It is December 1982.
I am to meet John Tripp in the Buffet car;
he will get on in Cardiff,
we will get out at Newport.

He is to talk, and read poems
to my writing class
at the Newport Unemployed People's Advice Bureau –
one floor of an old tax office
overlooking the bus station.

As we walk through town
John looks about him:
laughter at the sign HOROLOGIST
over a cheap jeweller's;
a shop-window in an arcade
displays glossy china fruit –
Is that nonsense still going on?
he bellows. The two assistants inside
look up. Further on
he says, *You can feel unemployment*
in these places. You can smell it.

The class met in an unused back room
which had a settee and some tube-and-canvas chairs.
There were no tables,
no electric plugs,
no heating
and no windows.
There was a firedoor that wouldn't close properly
and there was a crop of mushrooms on one wall.
Outside in the corridor someone is fiddling with a video.
John reads from his anti-nuclear sequence
THE ROAD FROM LOS ALAMOS.
Disarmament is still the most important issue
because it will affect our children
and their children as well.

The world remains *at the mercy of nervous men.*
The private seems to matter less and less
if I dwell on calamity.
The irrelevance of the lyric spirit –
Yeats and all that –
the private soul.

Most of the group were young and unemployed;
after the class we decide to have a drink.
In the street it is darker and colder,
and it's the night of a Welsh Cup-tie
so the cafes are closing early
and the pubs aren't going to open at all.
The town is full of people leaving
and policemen cloaked against the wind.
The Wimpy Bar's open, so we have coffee,
and then walk some way out of the centre
to an Irish bar down an alley.

There'll always be a place for conviviality,
says John over a pint and a whisky;
and, true, we are having a good time.
Someone mentions Samuel Beckett.
Have I got Beckett right? says John,
He thinks it's all shit – is that it?
You don't look like a poet, says someone else.
No, I look more like a retired army colonel.
Don't I? He laughs, and,
rubbing his unshaven chin,
leaves us to judge for ourselves.

Walk tonight

Walk tonight
    to Llandaff along the river
Everything shooting up
        New fingers of horse chestnut
          In the meadow,
    first dandelions
In the pub,
        Valleys voices
        That's a religious pint
           A good collar
The generations
    Old men
existed in big realities
        Coal   Steel   Chemicals
Innocent   Strong   Helpless
    Short, plump men
Heart problems
        in their flushed faces
And the women
    knitting fierce families
All different now
        It's different for the kids now

Walk back
    under the cathedral
recovering with the Spring
        Catching up, a slow process
The limes will soon be out
    How tell you?
        Why?
          Walk home by
St Teilo's Well, an owl
    hoots, no matter what
pinnacled pile they put here
        it's still a sacred spot
Moon and one planet
    New leaves shine in street light
In all the deep chords
        the details are important

Loneliness begets
    the need to speak
Not everyone feels this
      Lonely only children
        you and I
together now
    in our ways
still asking
      where does it all fit together?
Scenes glimpsed through lit evening windows
    THE STRUGGLE IS MY LIFE
      a poster under 50's radio on a shelf
        Next door
      an old man playing an accordion
In the street
    kids, arms round each other, singing

LEAP YEAR'S DAY 1992

> *...I make*
> *myself a bourbon and commence*
> *to write one of my 'I do this I do that'*
> *poems in a sketch pad.*
>   - Frank O'Hara, *GETTING UP AHEAD OF SOMEONE (SUN)*

A Saturday, damp under
   irrepressible light in the west

It's not just Spring
               is it?
I feel myself
        do I?
           quickening
I feel the nation
         are they?
              doing likewise
                    I hope
crawling out from under the burden

I walk
I walk to the bank machine
through the ragged-trousered consumers of Cowbridge Rd.
I walk to the stationer's
but they don't have any A4 bound notebooks
   worth buying. Too expensive
     or too boring.
       I look at filing cabinets.
       I buy
some typewriter paper & a pen.
I take my coat to the cleaner's.
I buy cigarettes.
I buy apples & bananas & sprouts.
I come home &
         unload.

I walk again,
through Pontcanna, Victorian
legacy,
     windowboxes, cats, alleys, olives.
No fresh pasta.

I buy Jakobson's *SOUND AND MEANING*
in the boring new second-hand bookshop
   noting the owner's Doppler Shift as he brays his vowels
   at his only other customer
& I buy *MODERN EUROPEAN VERSE*, ed. Dannie Abse,
1964 Pocket Poets edition,
a sliver of internationalism
   for the upcoming '60's.

It's raining.
It's not raining.
I walk down Kings Rd. to the Italian deli,
& still
      no fresh pasta.
I am directed.
I walk through Riverside
& down Clare St., fording social zones
   from stripped pine to wet rot,
     a different Victorian legacy,
       pausing only
under the railway bridge.

I buy fresh pasta
         in Grangetown.
I buy
   Vintage Gold cider, a tin of tomatoes
& a pork pie
      on the way back.
Then I buy
  an A4 sharp-cornered notebook
   in the *ART GALLERY*
where the sharp old lady & I
    consider the weather
     from all angles.
Miserable, but we need it.
The notebook-makers of China
have abandoned lurid blue covers
in favour of nebulaic marbling,
but they're still only £2.30.

Finally I buy grapes.
  I get home,
    feed the cats,

have food, cider, a joint, open
   MODERN EUROPEAN VERSE
    at Brecht,
     TO PROSPERITY:
Truly, the age I live in is bleak,
The guileless word is foolish.

THE BALLAD OF LYNETTE AND PINEAPPLE

Lynette was a working girl,
   working night and day.
Pineapple was her boyfriend,
   he loved her, in his way.

She stood outside the Custom House,
   in the cold and rain,
she gave her man the money
   to keep him in cocaine.

She stood outside the Custom House
   from lunchtime until late,
long after all the other girls
   had given up the wait.

The other girls would all go home,
   the Custom House would close,
Lynette would still be standing there
   to feed Pineapple's nose.

He slapped her when he'd done a line,
   he wanted more and more.
One day she'd simply had enough
   and walked out of the door.

.

She used a room in James Street,
   it only had a bed.
She lay down, and her worries
   went round and round in her head.

She couldn't go home to her father,
   he knew she was on the game.
He knew she lived with a black man;
   did she have no shame?

Pineapple would be looking
   to get back what was his.
She knew the state he'd be in,
   desperate for some whizz.

He'd be asking in the Custom House,
   asking all he met;
he'd ask the girls in the North Star
   if they'd seen Lynette.

She looked back to her childhood,
   she saw the road ahead.
No man will ever love me,
   not until I'm dead.

She dreamed she went out walking
   to St Agatha's well.
St Agatha was dressed in grey
   with two loaves and a bell.

Lynette held up a doll that came
   from Santa long ago,
but it fell in the filthy water
   far down below.

An owl was hooting on a branch
   Help me, help me please!
I am a lost soul unavenged;
   help me be released.

She woke alone, she prayed aloud,
   but she was unaware
the grace she sought for Pineapple
   was also hers to share.

It was the eve of Valentine,
   when she went out again;
she thought she'd do some business
   then get on that early train.

She stood upon a strange street,
   a car slowed down at last.
She took him back to James Street;
   she hoped to do him fast.

He prattled on like every man
   about his kids and wife.
She reached down for a condom,
   he came at her with the knife.

Fifty seven slashes,
   face and throat and breast;
he hacked away her womanhood
   in his frenzied quest.

She reached up to the window,
   she tried to give a cry,
her hand slid down the window,
   a bloody goodbye.

She reached up to the window,
   she gave a choking yell,
her hand slid down the window,
   a bloody farewell.

He delved deep to uncover
   what was making him insane.
Her organs didn't contain it;
   it was only in his brain.

He was trying to escape
   what was feasting on his soul,
but only Jesus Christ can die
   to make another whole.

And Christ is hanging from his Cross,
   our Saviour and our King,
at the other end of Bute Street.
   All life is suffering.

.

Time is obliterating
   the world that Lynette knew;
the Custom House has gone now,
   and the North Star too.

Cardiff Bay is booming,
   the Welsh Assembly's there,
lots of posh apartments,
   café-bars with fancy fare.

The developers were worried
   that all this low-life stuff
would stop the yuppies buying
   if they thought it was too rough.

Tiger Bay and old Rat Island
   are now The Bay, at last;
local colour's good for sales
   if it's safely in the past.

So let's clear up this business,
   those crackheads aren't that tough;
Pineapple will admit his guilt
   if we ask him long enough.

We've even got some witnesses
   although they seem confused
(but with these type of people
   that'll be excused).

It seems that we can pin it on
   Pineapple and his mates;
Some cry *Unsafe convictions*!
   but that'll soon abate.

The Bay must be a safe place,
   that should be our goal,
where a man can take his wife and kids
   for an ice-cream and a stroll.

OLD LADY WITH MOTOR NEURONE DISEASE

Have I become
hard? Do I
really care,
tonight, up in
the council estate?

I'm not a baby
I think she says
through drooled vowels,
to justify
her panic attacks
at the hospital tests.
It's just she can't
lie down - she even sleeps
sitting up, interprets
her daughter.
She attempts
a bovine cough,
larynx filling up
behind a tongue like
the Sargasso,
eel-sack fasciculation.

She'll be dead
soon. I never quite
get used to that feeling.

Outside, I'd
forgotten how high up
it is here,
unusual elevation
for Cardiff.
What am I
doing here? Looking
east beyond
hedges, dogs,
boarded up shops,
huddled people,
through sharp sleet
to the grey hills
of Gwent.

THE CAR PARK

...a nothing that is yet an infinity
smallest hint of a germ of a blossom

- Harmony Poem to Han-Shan
by Shih-Shu ('Stones And Trees')

When you lie in bed, in the autumn or winter or spring,
when you wake early, in the dark,
you can tell what time it is
by the surge of traffic coming into town
along Western Avenue and Cowbridge Road
and down Cathedral Road, boundaries of the settlement
west of the river, the Canna, now underground
tracked by willows by the old Canton workhouse
(Over the hill to the Union), and the diagonal passage
of Neville Street towards the Taff and then
through the tamed, barraged, unmuddy Bay
into the Severn.
              Attend! The traffic starts
gently, intermittently, from near silence, building
to a steady roar, with heavier undertones
of buses, lorries, the police helicopter,
and higher themes of car alarms, and ambulance wails
as people wake up dying.
              Listen! In late winter
there's the thrush, hesitant at first,
by the old stone market-garden wall,
practising, building his confidence, in the dark,
in the cold, in the rain.
              Hear! The mocking cackle
of gulls, wheeling and squabbling and chuckling
in their time, one of their times, dawn, pre-dawn,
swooping down to unpeel urban roadkill,
fast food remains fetid in flattened wax-packs
and polystyrene on the tarmac and in the car park,
the boxed souls of battery chickens
transmigrating to freedom.
              The car park!
The backs of shops and the ghosts of streets and buildings

demolished in its making. Avon Street
off Severn Road, previously Halket Street
(Halket: The large grey seal *Halichoerus grypus*,
forebear of Billy the Seal, who escaped from Victoria Park
in a flood, and swam down Cowbridge Road, stopping
for fish and chips and a pint of dark on the way).
The Crown, still standing in unsplendid isolation,
once the corner pub, now an estate agent's
worried by the effect of car torchings on house prices.
A Canton barbecue: *I saw a man pull up in a car,*
he got out and just threw something into the back seat.
Mindless! But we're not all bad round here...
Flashing lights, firemen, tow-trucks, a good crowd.
Next day, a burnt patch, sharp crumbs of glass and
small metal bits among the other rubbish -
leaflets ripped from under windscreen wipers
by irritated drivers, *Eat What You Like And*
Still Lose Pounds, Why Pay High Street Prices,
Earn From Home, All day Breakfast,
SALSA DANCING!
        Dumped mattresses,
drums of old cooking oil, used needles
and condoms
        And the auditory rubbish,
hand-brake screeches, car alarms - urban cicadas.
        Early
every Friday morning (in termtime) for 15 years
the poet walked through the car park, on his way home
to the hills, scanning the sky for sparrowhawks.
Has anyone else noticed this?
        And in the early evenings,
people sorting through rubbish bags removed
from outside charity shops - Look, for instance,
at that fireside set with no poker thrown down by the wall -
a companion set with no companions,
turned out by its owners, rejected by the Heart Foundation,
cast aside even by ragpickers!
        But I have seen
this car park in ecstasy, one febrile magic dawn
as I walked towards Hamilton Street.
        And in spring
the tree in the car park flowers! In its square
of kerbed grass, pissed on by all the dogs, unfit for service,

a non-combatant in the Battle Of The Trees, left in the rear
by the brigades of limes lining the streets,
the horse-chestnuts with flower-cones stiff in their
new fingers marching across Pontcanna Fields,
the giant pines of Rookwood Arboretum,
the oaks of St Fagans - even the car park tree,
a Council tree in a Council car park, has
small, creamy, unnoticed flowers. Look! See!
                                        See too,
in spring and summer, the Asian lads
between prayers at the mosque, playing cricket -
no parks round here - light evenings of bat and ball
and orange-crate wicket, hitting fierce and
shouting out and diving to the floor, a trade-off
between glory and Weil's Disease - No contest!

JAMES STREET

Don't look for the love of innocence in a port
- Ko Un, 'Song Of Innocence'.

Park by the Sally Army in Grangetown
Cross the Taff, cross-
   currents blown by cold wind
      forming diamonds in watery counterpoint

New flats lining the river
back of Dumballs Rd

Tacky silver lighthouse like a stove-pipe
on rocks outside the new Police Station -
some secure cells in there, I hear -
words carved on the rocks, *You're busted*
in every language known to man,
says Mick

            The White Hart
where we once heard a man do the drum part
from *Night In Tunisia* on a back bar-table
until threatened with eviction by the 3 Irish women
who ran the place

            And the Somali
Community Centre and the old Hip & Pil,
the Ship & Pilot's busted sign as it was
for years – now a revolving sequence of
over-optimistic bistros and forgettable cafe-bars

Abandoned building on the right,
buddleia and pigeons, marvellous mosaic
of decay on the rendering

The Nonpareil Market arch

Steelwork skybox of a half-built block, corner of
West Bute St by Mick and Joan's,
good view of the massage parlour from their new flat

opposite bookmaker's and rooms above
where Lynette was slashed to death

Now we're drawn across emptiness, sieved through
the automatic teeth of the heavy-browed golden whale,
plankton ingested into the too-big foyer of the
Millennium Centre, where box-office girls are clueless
about any exhibition but suggest a first-floor walkway

Yes – photos by Harry Hammond, Britain's
leading showbiz photographer, 1950's and '60's,
birth of rock & roll days. Great pictures! But here in the
bright grey corridor it's not that energy itself but
the memory of energy

                    Coffee
in the cafe overlooking the boarded-over quay,
sole occupant of the amphitheatre a dog chasing a ball
joyfully

        Then we go out to stand under
your favourite sculpture, tall mirrorslab
with water cascading down, slow flow, and
our fluid shapes barely there behind the waterfall.

AUTUMN 1990

I.M. Ruby Pillar &
Lawrence Hills

Words are not the truth

Truth is direct seeing

    (whilst Image replaces Substance
                          everywhere

        Maps   &   Mud)

I'm still here
          now & then

approaching autumn
the gusty deaths of my conception-month

The Image:
        of a dying lioness
licking passionately at the grass
as her haunches shudder in long spasms

Ambiguity of death
Dualities

      .

Some leaves have fallen

      .

We could be in London today
   walking clockwise round the Square
   re-marking the changes in that little world
   a damper, quieter place
     but we're not.

Instead, it's unadmitted conflicts
& the tension of trying to escape them
Waking at 12.45 with a thumping hangover
& now it's a soggy Sunday afternoon
like Sundays in the 50's
cabbage & Unchained Melody seeping through the walls.

.

Death
Awkward feelings to do with *self*
What is it?
The lack of the person very real
The Image
          of the person
freed from their handicap
- flying? -
as they sometimes were in life?
Some kind of haze of motion, an emanation
from all the parts
A process
          not separate

& this self often
destroyed prior to death
Pain, stroke, progressive
    disintegration, confusion, delusion
Suffering is a variation of the problem of evil
To thicken the plot is OK
    if someone's there
to appreciate the subtlety

The lioness
licking passionately at the grass

The Image
          doesn't need to be beautiful
it needs to be
          inevitable

The poverty of the Image
allows exploration
                  & involvement

   Purity

      .

I have been in the outer edges
of my nation, my patch, my
place - Hafrenia? - Sabrinia? -
across the Levels, up Valleys
in praise of dark skies
   with a rainbow
      white birds
         white upturned leaves
      blown against them

This is still a place

On the Welsh side
   over the Usk
24 foot tidal fall
revealing smelly mud
studded with supermarket trolleys

To the north first
   snow on the hills

VALLEY OF THE ROCKS

What I bring

and what you bring

and what's HERE

The compulsion

of perception

Dead trees

breeding monsters

The mind's a hunter of forms

Venator formarum

And histories

Past the lurch-backed side-slewed church

along the deep lane

under the Graig

Valley of the Rocks

Temenos

Arena

Ferns and sheep runs

Sloes and little stony summits

of ash trees on cliff rubble

Rockfall hollow

Origins/Creations:

Landslip at the whip end

of the quake line?

Marcle Hill

Dorstone

Skirrid

Valley of the Yoke

Notch of the Graig

Or lightning-struck hill-cleft?

Or the rending

of Heaven and Earth

in the darkness of the Crucifixion?

The deflected chancel

The moon turned to blood

Raven hassling

a peregrine

up on the cliff

Peaks and waves and

troughs

Clear spot

for a trip

Hatterall

Allt-yr-Haul

Toward the Sun

Pointing the only way

Beyond my questions

Before my answers

To change

To open

To maintain

To remember

the present

and yes to remember

love's face

Sun-face

To tread

light

To watch

the details

I.M. T. Leary

Cheerleader for evolution

And for the Centenary

of David Jones' birth

I have looked for a long while

at the textures and contours

Cwmyoy

above Llanthony, '96

DRIVING A FRIEND BACK TO THE HILLS, & PICKING SLOES

For C.T.

I love you again, old friend
Your illumination by the Steam Laundry

Replacing a lost faith
A whole life

Integrity
A steady purpose

You are thankful
& so am I

With a gift of carrots
we leave you at the cottage door

A passionate autumn
Sere - is that the sound?

Gold light on the Fans
Dark sky behind   Chill wind

Picking sloes from a small tree
by the road over the Common

Climbing on a low stone wall
to reach the thickest clusters

Sheep behind their wire look up
Blue bums, served by the ram

Mrs B. at the shop
thinks these are bullaces

but the round, ripe-bloomed fruit
is small, & the tree

is black-twigged
with sharp spines!

Upland fruit
Astringent   Enough

to half fill a large kilner jar
Add a palmful of almonds

Drown it all deep in gin
Shake daily

GLYNMERCHER, DEC. '01

Freezing hard
  subtle glitter
    shadows
and light on snow -
   full moon
     (slipper full of snow)
    Farm dogs barking in the night

From THE PRESS OF SILENCE

A WALK TO PATRICIO
for Graham Hartill

PROLOGUE: PRUNING THE VINE

December: cold day,
bright in Cardiff
but cloudy in the hills.

The pond frozen.
Pruning the vine
all the way back

to the central, tough stem.
Still a few grapes
in the greenhouse

among the blare
of autumn vine leaves.
North, the spurs of Gader

and the clouds clearing
to small pale fans
against blue.

Carrying the prunings
to be burnt, we both stop
to view the sky

and plan a walk up there
later in the year
      to Patricio.

THE WELL

   June: Scrambling down through the Forestry, and along the
green lane above Grwyne Fawr, we see a wheatear (white-arse),
an upturned tree with rocks clutched in its roots and foxgloves
round it, two dead lambs (one caught in a wire fence), and rut-

puddles reflecting us: Graham and Finn the red dog and I.

And now we see steep little red-marl fields and isolated farms across the valley. We come across the steep metalled road suddenly, by a sheep fold; and, equally suddenly, Patricio church itself, through a stone stile in the churchyard wall, next to a large guelder rose in full flower. We carry on down the hill. To the left, a path by a trickle of water, Nant Mair, Mary's Brook.

Here at the well lived Issui the Martyr, Merthyr Ishow, Silurian saint, who hospitably received a traveller, entertained him in his humble cell, and this thankless guest murdered him. Issui, did you see Death coming, was your heart quiet and at ease? Was your body stuffed down the well? What was the motive? Why rob a man with nothing? Was it day or was it night? Did you wish you could give him that full moon too?

THE LYCH GATE

The classic view - irresistible -
frames the church
in the lych gate's arch.
This is the upward angle taken
in a painting of Patricio
by the wife of Doug, a man
struck speechless by a stroke.
She gave me the picture
as a thank you for the work
- little enough! - I'd done
with the dyspraxic Doug.
In truth, the painting was a bit
wooden in execution, but
accurate, and heartfelt.

I hung it in the office,
which was a drab, untended place.
When I moved from that job
I left the picture behind.
One of my colleagues
thought I was just dumping it,
so I explained
its history to her.

If it means so much to you
why not take it with you?
How could I tell her
it was just because
it meant so much
that I was leaving it?

IN THE CHURCH

The fenestrated rood-screen, silver-grey
unpainted oak on a breastsummer beam,
has foliated trails of vines and grapes
being devoured by - or else sprouting from -
a dragon's mouth. The network of the stems
and leaves makes a prolific tracery...

     a natural human response
     to the riotous growth
     in the cwm below

Opposite the door
the figure
of Death/Time -
life-size skeleton
in red ochre (allegedly
unscrubbable blood) -
heart-in-a-barrel ribs, holding

    scythe

       spade

          hourglass

  reap

      dig

         Hurry up please it's...

...in gradual manner you become aware
(and that awareness can be frightening)

it's Death that sits beside you on the mat;
at ease, with quiet heart, you serve the guest.

The saint's skin

nailed to the door

in memory.

AN ALCOHOLIC GETTING THE BUM'S RUSH FROM TESCO'S

A guy
     waiting in line for the checkout
2 bottles on the belt
        & a tenner on top of his
loyalty card

OK, he's unshaven & unstylish
     & can't keep still –
looks around, slow to register, quick to
        look paranoid –

chronic Korsakoff's
     (which sounds
more like a vodka than a
        syndrome)

The checkout woman
     presses a hidden bell
The security guard
       smooches his mobile

The manager discusses the problem
     with the guard calmly and quietly
backs turned on the guy
       & when he gets to the till

they won't serve him
     Why? he asks
Because you're already drunk
       You've had enough

says the manager politely but
     masterfully
Alright says the guy
      I'll go

and he leaves – no trouble –
      with his hands up in surrender
as if being arrested rather than released
        into blank freedom

Sorry about that says the checkout woman
        to the next customer
& the manager and the guard watch him go
        & then walk off

But where was the evidence
      of his acute inebriation?
Given his chronic state
        he did very well

to put the bottles flat on the moving belt
      so they didn't get jerked & fall over
& he even remembered
        his loyalty card

Memory
      Forward planning
Hand-eye co-ordination
        Surely

on any cognitive test
      yet devised
he merited his rightful place
        among the consumers?

FIXING THE LIGHT

(After Iain Sinclair's LANDOR'S TOWER)

Gwain arrives Thursday night as usual
with Boston Ale and a small triangular packet
We chat – as usual – round the fire
Smoke   Drink   Give delayed 60th birthday pres
A new Italian coffee pot
Next morning it's a Full English
then off to Glynmercher
via Tesco's for rice & wine & coffee
& the Ty Nant under Garth Wood –
a Cardiff power spot –
for 2 pts of Rev. James

It's bright but cold
& a slow journey
through roadworks at Mountain Ash
Usual parking spots closed
for foot & mouth
so we tuck the car in on the verge
by a small hawthorn bush
walk through the field gate
& spray shoes with disinfectant

At the cottage Gwain lights the fire
then we pull the woodboxes out the way
& push the sofa back
The surface of the wooden chest
is cleared of papers & typewriter
& the chest is positioned
under the light
Filo turns off the wall switch
& opens the fusebox
We debate which is the right fuse
& bet on the white-spotted one
which proves to be correct
since the study light doesn't come on either
when power's switched back on

Switch it off again
Gwain aims the torch
Jean climbs on the chest & cuts
the old shade free –
square wire frame with coloured wool round it
from hippy days of early 70's
smothered in dusty cobwebs

Remove light bulb
The only problem is the collar
round the fitting, which falls apart
with the removal of the bulb
Get new fitting purchased by Gwain
in Swansea market – he was assured
this was *just what was needed* –
& screw onto original fitting
having first put new charity shop
pleated plastic shade on upside down
to form an uplight
Replace bulb
Replace fuse
Turn power on
Turn wall switch on
Light works
Bright beam directed upwards
by umbelliferous new shade
Cobwebs further up on the ceiling-fitting
dance with joy
Put cover back on fuse box
Shake hands all round
Replace furniture
Total running time two minutes
thirty five seconds for
entire operation
Nobody died
Make coffee in new coffee pot
Sit by fire under new light
and drink it

YR HEN EGLWYS SS 876809

for Val

Sunny, warm

       but with a pallid quality

              to the blue of the sky -

autumn coming.

       First, to Bridgend,

              Tesco for diesel,

McDonalds for a

       pee. Then Laleston,

              dormitory village,

up a narrow lane,

       high hedges,

              to a minor junction.

There they are, behind

       nettles & grasses,

              the 2 stones!

We park up the lane

       under a big ash

              by some balsam in flower

& an old car battery

     & a dead TV.

        The way in, the approach,

which might once have been

     a field gate,

        is also impeded – soggy

mattresses, smashed

     kitchen units.

        The stones, a male

& a female lozenge,

     are six feet high,

        six apart,

heads up above

     the nettles & bushes.

        They're facing each other,

talking to each other

     for all I know

        about staying true & close

in old age,

     their only hope

        in a crazy, ugly

world. No sign

of old walls or any

remains of a building;

on the male stone,

the suggestion of a cross.

Above them, on a rise

up the slightest of tracks,

is the view north

over rough fields

to the Services & Retail Park

on the motorway at Sarn.

FFYNON FAIR, PENRHYS

A stone hut
    above the Rhonddas
below the roundabout

Padlocked iron fence
    Pilgrims' patio
2 supermarket trolleys
    Some struggling daffs

      Glimpse of a trough
        inside:
            a pin well
      to sharpen the eyes

        A pin in place of gold
    A strip of cloth
      for animal sacrifice

    The water squeezed out
        between the strata
    Pennant series
        overlying the Coal Measures

    Hospice and shrine
        Property of the white monks
    down in Llantarnam
        Offerings of alms and a taper

1538: Mary
    nursing Jesus
  for a kiss
      taken down by night
and burnt in London
  A jolly muster

In régime-change
    go for the statues:

  Saddam's head
      swung onto a lorry

  Stalin's ear
      now a paddling pool

    and the Taliban at Bamiyan
      blasting Buddhas
  with tanks, mortars and artillery

At Smithfield
    the oaken image
  blue and gold
      drowns in fire
unflinching

At Penrhys
    the water
  trickles on
      down the hill

PICTURES OF PILL

TAXI office
  Torn sofa
outside

Curtain hanging out
  through smashed window

Upturned traffic cone

      It's the sunshine that foregrounds
      the dereliction, not the bleaker rain:
      walking under the railway bridge
      along the new dual-carriageway
      that's sliced off the terraced streets

The market
  packing up
Fat boy carries
  loud rolls of cloth

THE TOP OF THE RANGE CLUB

      Hazy, tired, febrile; a certain stillness
      in the heat. You don't get it so much
      in Cardiff now, the muddy bay,
      the empty warehouses, the rampant,
      dusty weeds, all gone for marinas,
      apartments, sponsored roundabouts

Demolished building
  first floor
rusty stove
  in a niche

The old
  Police Station
Flame car
  DEVIL'S PROJECT

Newport's still just about like that,
edging the slacklands of summer

Transporter bridge
   rising up
between 2 houses

DYFFRYN GARDENS AND ST LYTHANS

Dyffryn: current house built in 1893. The gardens are Edwardian, coinciding with the commercial 'heyday' of Cardiff.

St Lythans: megalithic chamber tomb or dolmen, between 3700-3300 BC. One of the Cotswold-Severn group of tombs. Geographical subdivision: the Glamorgan and Monmouthshire coastal group, including sites on Gower, and Tinkinswood. Terminal chambers.

Early views on the history of this group of tomb-builders stressed the similarity of the transepted chamber plan to those in Western France and saw them as colonisers from France moving up the Severn Estuary. More recently, the complexity of their architectural inspiration has led to the view that the unique mixture of influences occurred within Britain, combining the formality of earthen long barrow mound design with at least two traditions of continental chamber architecture. Such an amalgam would most likely have been fused in the Cotswolds and Wiltshire, with the Welsh examples representing a secondary expansion (Frances Lynch *et al*, PREHISTORIC WALES, 2000, p. 67).

ANNALS OF SOUTH GLAMORGAN, by Marianne Robertson Spencer (circa 1914, p. 173) has a photograph and says that there is a hole through the end stone through which it was suggested that the spirit of the departed was supposed to take flight when his remains had been deposited in their last earthly home.

Marvellous stones with indentations, holes, and variegated lichen. *Pelvic spirit holes. Lichen handprints.*

'Trepanning' of the skull was supposed to release the demon or spirit causing problems. Skull attack. This is *lithotrepanning*. Lithotrepanation..

The lichen 'handprints' on the stones have the suggestion of 'fish tails' at the 'wrist'.

A large replica of St Lythans Megalithic chamber, in Radyr stone, was constructed in front of the Prince of Wales Hospital for Limbless Sailors and Soldiers, to mark its opening in 1918. The Hospital (now flats) was off Richmond Road in Roath. The

replica, which has a spirit hole, was donated by Miss Cory of
Dyffryn House.

TINKINSWOOD

Capstone: 22 feet by 3 feet thick. Weighs 40 tons. Drystone
walling: the horizontal dry-walling is original; the herringbone
walling dates from the 1914 excavations.

R.E.M. Wheeler (1925) mentions the old belief that anyone
who slept within the dolmen on a spirit night would suffer one
of the following calamities – he would either die, go raving mad
or become a poet.

On a brick support-pier at Tinkinswood is written
EXCAVATED 1914. Shortly after this, it is probable that many of
those involved in the 'excavation' were excavating trenches in
France. Tinkinswood is Cardiff's most poignant war memorial,
given the ironies of time – the terminal chambered tomb, the
French origin of the design, the innocent opening of the tomb in
1914.

(Heard on the radio: there are 37,000 war memorials in
Britain, of many different types, commemorating 750,000 named
dead, reflecting *a pall of grief* over Britain in the 20th Century.
Tinkinswood isn't one of them.)

I first went to St Lythans, Tinkinswood, and to the
Druidstone at Michaelstone-y-Fedw, to the east of Cardiff, in
1975. The Druidstone is a single standing stone, a half-buried
feminine lozenge about ten feet high, now in a private garden.
Of course, there is a legend about it: that when a cock crows at
midnight, the stone uproots itself and goes for a swim in the
river.

BOTANISING AT WEST ABERTHAW

On the beach

    concrete cubes –

- anti-tank defences

      undermined – tilting

        at crazy angles –

and smashed, so you can see

    how they were made –

pattern of board shuttering,

    concrete on the outside,

      large beach stones inside,

        angle iron for

          reinforcement

- one gashed open, a cave

    of herbrobert

Long lines of them,

    derailed boxcars boxcars boxcars –

      chuffing me off to Dachau

Some you can walk on

    like a path -

      looks like JARROW

inscribed in one –

    anyone alive

        who worked on these?

Echoed by haybales

    stacked up in the field behind –

rectangles not cottonreels –

        the lost summers of WW2

A green tractor with yellow wheels

      Ragwort in front of the power station

        The beach

            lush & barren

    shoes & crates & driftwood &

                doll limbs

      Yarrow in front of the power station

Low sloes

    flat to stones

        Thistle, hawkweed, fennel in front of

    the power station

        & look – there it is,

    pink seedhead, white flowers,

      Parsley Water Dropwort!

AUTUMN, SULLY-BARRY

Stinking iris
grinning red,
   cliff trees & bushes
     wind-shaped

Smell of seaweed,
smell of salt
   like a lover's
     licked skin

Low tide on
the jumble-slab beach,
   fishermen
     all in a line

yet each alone
with tripod & line
   each bent
     to his task

like a lone gull
like that small boat
   out on the
     misty water

Walk from the slipway...

Walk from the slipway at Sully
to Barry. Today's only colour
the scarlet-tooth pods of
stinking iris, grinning at the easterly
from under the skeleton hedge
black-boned thicket edging
the slippery beach
between the docks
& the chemical works
sea & sky integrating
behind freighters & small islands
moored in the channel
Gale sway   soft strata
cracked concrete   fences
falling into nothing
A man, a woman and a child
round a fire on the stones

NOTES

AUTUMN 1990

Ruby Pillar – a handicapped friend.

Lawrence Hills – founder of the Henry Doubleday Research Association; organic gardener.

The image of the dying lioness is from Peter Matthiessen's *THE TREE WHERE MAN WAS BORN* (1972). Readers wishing to draw parallels with events in British politics in November 1990 may do so.

'...walking clockwise round the Square' – The Square is Eccleston Square in Victoria, London. Students from the Buddhist Society take meditative exercise – *kinhin* – around the Square at lunchtimes. The garden in the centre of the Square, 'that little world/a damper, quieter place', was renovated by a committee chaired by the photographer Roger Phillips, and is fertilised by spent hops from Young's Wandsworth Brewery.

Who was it who, when asked why there was evil in the world, replied, *To thicken the plot?*

CARDIFF VARIATIONS:

AN AFTERNOON AND EVENING WITH JOHN TRIPP

This poem in memory of John Tripp is set in Newport rather than Cardiff, but I always think of him as being *the old poet of the city*, as Lawrence Durrell described Cavafy and Alexandria. John certainly wasn't old, however, when he died aged 58 in 1986.

THE BALLAD OF LYNETTE AND PINEAPPLE

The area around the Custom House pub, where the 20-year-old Lynette White stood waiting for punters, is now an empty, windy space with a vandalised stained-glass fountain. After a long campaign, the Cardiff Three, including Stephen 'Pineapple' Miller, have been released from prison and exonerated of murder. *The Ballad Of Lynette And Pineapple* was written during that campaign. The man subsequently convicted of killing Lynette White on St Valentine's Day 1988 turned out to be nothing like my imagined portrait of him.

THE CAR PARK
For those unfamiliar with Cardiff, Canton (Treganna in Welsh) is an inner city suburb to the west of the city. Its name derives from its position on the Canna, a minor tributary of the Taff.

THE PRESS OF SILENCE
The church at Patricio, in the Black Mountains, was built in memory of the hermit-saint Issui, murdered by a traveller to whom he'd given hospitality. The wall-painting of Death/Time is a medieval *memento mori*. Thanks to the late Ven. Myokyo-ni, and to H. J. Massingham's *THE SOUTHERN MARCHES* (1952).

YR HEN EGLWYS
sarn (-au) nf causeway; nm litter, ruin, destruction.
Collins Welsh Dictionary.

PICTURES OF PILL
Pill – Pillgwenlly, docks area of Newport.

BOTANISING AT WEST ABERTHAW
'chuffing me off to Dachau' – Sylvia Plath, 'Daddy'.

AUTUMN, SULLY-BARRY
The line *'like a lover's/licked skin'* is stolen from Trezza Azzopardi – 'The smell of the foreshore, of a lover's licked skin', from *THE HIDING PLACE* (Picador, 2000).

CHRIS TORRANCE

The New Territory

In transit Bristol – Wales, June 1970

The warm, turbulent wind
rushes wildly across the flat limestone plain
Couples grope & stir in the sun
thigh hooked over thigh they embrace
moving restlessly on the short turf
over the hard, baked ground
A zephyr picking up winged tree seeds
whirls them over the wrapt, hot bodies
of the lovers lying there
The clear, bland air:
the skin-blistering sun

Up to Abercarn & Mountain Ash & Aberdare
one long terraced Main St with pitheads & coking plants

the red & green phantoms leap across the fall

a butterfly alights briefly on the meniscus
to drink before flying off

the magic glass swayed by a ripple
– within the instant of its thought
comes birthing at the surface, at the rib-point
a life of no more deception, of no more lies!

'& continued to the Rhymney pub for a few pints
through misty rain'
the dripping oak avenue
'& mountains only bloom in the autumn'

Quintessential day

Lying in corners of the room
the books get slung like leaves
too many iron-browed teachers of the law
Your cosmology & mine are
by far the most interesting subjects, & the most fun
to explore, & that I would
much rather try to be shapeless;
iras, in extinction of.
The heavy, secret lies of the heart.
Black raven wings brushing the sky,
impacting air, fade slowly,
beating in the blood.

Aries
for Andi

I stare at the rams in the fields
& in the intervals sawing logs
these ethereal conversations will have to stop
I listen to the song of the saw
or the warbling of the hallucinatory chaffinch
the grain of spirit stirred

journeyed to the sacred spring
the landscape fluctuating in changing light
– her hands make out of air
tapestries of motion, all talk of 'mildness'
abnegated by the initial burst,
thrilling to the equinoctial summit.

slow tractors spreading muck in the distant dun fields
the mystery that roils in the blood
sitting around talking ourselves back down
through gradually quieting waves.

Midsummer Sun Declining

The streams shallow or gone in this dry month
the dawn chorus equally reduced to a token trickle
the dog days
await
the temblor, the undammed current
this waiting
the land   dry

seed capsules, triggers
adrift upon the airflow   the kestrel shimmers
his wings, soaring   coming to anchor in the sky

writing by candlelight
the most ancient strobe of man
his firelight
tales of the ancestors
perpetuation   myth   identity

the faces of many friends pass before me in dreamy procession

I am so many people   I am not   I am everybody else
but in singular order, not in plurality
I see myself as vestiges, backdrops, moods, images, casts

poets kick their feet around the place & fertilize the queen
the old poet drones, the old pranksters, lurking around with
a sly fiddle & a little ditty air

the moon so slow!   the deep summer moon!
the bull gibbering & slavering on the slope at dawn
rubbing his prick up against some tree stump in frustration

swathes of mist stand up still under the trees

the planet Mars travelling under a cinnamon moon

Irregular Sonnet

The whaleback of the grim mountain
that is always so black in the South
turned shades of jade & slate green
by this cold wind that has come
from a cold land, lightly salting
the tops with snow

     an industrial city smokes & glazes
in the gaps to the SW

     until man has spread enough of his grease over the land
to gain himself a place, a homestead

smell the stinks blowing up the valley from Swansea
your tension isn't alone in the guilty, miscellany night

     the stillness of snow
sleeping on mountain tops

The Sparrowhawk
for Jean McIntosh

As I came round the side of the house,
climbing over the stone stile, a sparrowhawk!
said Val, from the bedroom window, & sure enough
there it was, had cornered a wren in a thorn bush,
over by the barn, & would sweep round the bush,
to frighten it out, but the wren having learnt,
after a couple of initial, heart-pumping chases,
that it was safer where it was, stayed put,
quavering, tremulous

        & the hawk almost desultory
        about the whole affair,
        would preen & ruffle a feather or two,
        then take off for another low-level flight
        round the bush, rounded wings
        splayed to the tips, tail down behind, anchoring

but after a few minutes, tiring of this
unfruitful exercise, it flew off, skimming
narrowly round the corner of the barn & into the gully,
where the grinding chatter of missle thrushes
soon revealed its activity there, hunting amongst the hazel & ash
& for some time after you could trace its progress
through the scrub woods, by the fuss & commotion,
a bowwave of alarm calls & trepidation, over the hedgerows,
& into the ravine beyond.

The Ice Saints of May

Cut an alder, saw a collie
at the carcase of an ewe
         dead in lamb birth

       sheep
voices in the fields all day long
haunt my footsteps
uttering the foodcall

lamb dives
shaking the ewe's frame as he
pulls lustily for milk

red rattle, bog cotton
& pimpernel

ghostly bracts of brake
unfurl their strength
in leafmouldy darkness

The Ice Saints of May
rear their anvilous heads
about the horizon

queen wasp flops
history bulging in her womb

Spinning the Poem

Concerned with the brew in the sky
the physics of that dimension, crucible
today I cut the bracken in the
small, North-sloping field
behind the barn, & there were
sticky flies & a frog or two

Peppery scent of
neon pink lupins
foundering in raindrops
calves look in the gate

I set to identify
patriarchs & scribes & buglers
amongst the herd
the bull sidles up behind
his fancy & laps a mouthful of urine

He makes sounds
in my head as I
press a flower in a book with a midge
a dried cadaver that falls out a year later

The House of Stone

The house of stone
stuck
like a worn and stubborn thumb
in the Glen of Mercury
buffeted by endless rainstorms

etched fabric of cross-birch
cross-thorn & cross-alder
mimicked by miniature frets
of lichen outgrowths
encrusted on
dead birch twigs

swinging amongst catkins in the fork of a hazel
is the wind-stripped corpse of a dog fox
hindquarters bared by weeks of galewash
the naked balls hanging pathetic between
thighs holed by death-blow or carrion creature

Large drops falling from the black branches
mud & water thrown out from the welts
with every step taken

the floodgates of the loving season

February filldyke
February sproutkale
February pointbulb

Overgrown straggly hedgerows, through which
many holes & gaps have been worn by browsing stock
            the land drains slowly bogging up
              wormy mud for the woodcock
              & snipe up on the common; each quag
            releasing its abundance of soupy habitat for
            demoiselle, frog, pondskater, water beetle,
                            rat-tailed maggot

            crowfoot, water plantain & forget-me-not;
            slippery green stones with caddises & tiny mussels
                            underneath

a wealth, a plethora, a foodchain

peregrine, takes the woodcock
fox, takes the woodcock
gun, takes the woodcock

      his feathers & bones melt into the soil

Nant Y Moch

At the confluence
of the Hanging Valley stream
with the River Nedd

our invocation
to the God of that triple point...

sat contemplating
this huge pile of rubbish on the other bank
that looked like it had been compiled
by a bulldozer
before realizing I was looking at
the side of the glacial moraine
into which the stream had cut

Who Was That Man

That little ritual
always makes the kettle boil
that sigh impugning upon
post-prandial languor
the bringing to a head of steam
you are running along the platform
the train is already moving
a man holds open the door for you
reaches for your suitcase
& pulls you inside
who was that man? & how many dreams
of escaping trains were you involved in
before you caught this one? & how do words
manage to lie so, this time
& as always? Words murder sleep
& then when you
sleep dreams murder you. The fiend pulling you
onto a giant hypodermic needle
protruding from his forehead
& during the day you go muttering round
'There is no way out' or
'There is no exit' but all the time
the trap is you, learning how to live with yourself
& finding learning painful & hard to come by, why,
you are that man! The only person who can
rescue you from yourself. In the meantime
we find the self wreckage on a foreign shore
& vision is suitably dimmed. This accounts for
a feeling of alienation within us
What we cant have & what you cant have etc.
This living dream of horror sleep. Or this
acid-lemon light, this gold & silver flowing
in the placid bulb's wattage, gentle white walls
going into smoky yellow, this
flame-coloured chair, this
slow-moving chorus of blue & purple flame
that sits wavering over the late coals
The hissing of the monsoon
becomes an echo of the placid black kettle
steaming water into the pot, swirl of rosemary leaves
that's to fix your memory, son.

Maen Madoc

The limestone pavement
partially submerged in
grassy humps

a few red sandstone erratics
ponder the retreat of the ice

After climbing several
drystone walls &
'characteristic rubbly gnolls'

there was the stone
a sentinel on
the high & lonely moor
set into the matrix
of the Roman way, Sarn Helen

          The Court Jester
          by his artistry
          influences affairs
          of state
          in the drenched lands
          where an unbroken
          dynasty of Kings
          stretches back
          to a lone
          standing stone
          on a bald-headed
          conical mountain

Circumnavigating the Mountain

The cycle
meanders
the perfect
poem

fox's mask
expressionless
glares up at me
from the gutter
mangled body
at Storey Arms

headwind
baffling my strength
sit by
Silurian erratic
menhir slab
laid on the fair turf
of Mynydd Illtyd

silkiest maritime
summer high
swirling breezes
the trees blurred washed out
cirrus tuffs moving up ahead in line

Boreas at my back
helps me up the cwm
at the head of Senni
to Maen Llia
rainspots dance in the
sunny cloudy wind

Subsidence Was Pulsatory, However

Red wink of sun
settling into hillside notch
a cloud of spinnerets
whirls from the sycamore
faint rain all day
trough subsiding weakly above
while leaves hang limp, or lie damp
in piled drifts; small bitter apples
rot under tree
in mounds of trampled dung,
sweet rotten stench
fermenting together
under the hooves of the cattle
who gather to eat them
picking them out
of the marshy terrain
eroding away downslope
exposing tree root thighs
reaching into ground
both manuring
& killing the tree

Bread rising on the hearth
progress of a large
staggery black beetle across the floor
logs make keening sounds
the very stones reach out
arms of soft wisdom & worldly knowledge
asleep in the drizzling rain
surrounded by bog & mud on all sides
or woody slope overhanging ravine
honeysuckle treerope clinging
to hawthorn bole
only the farmtrack
is known, safe ground
the little road climbs
by a hairpin out of Mercury
turns along the edge &
surveys awhile the valley

heaving in abeyant colour
a myriad small birds flock over
tossing & turning in expert flight
individual chases through the pack
a gate clangs between two stones
tufty little mounds lead onto the
peat-watery common
hen harrier quietly quartering
low over ground disappearing
merging into distance & background
imagine being a sheep
puddling constantly through this
quagmire. Welsh mountain sheep
really are tough
as is winter-resistant curly kale
springily resilient to my teeth today.

A roadwork
cut into subsoil
outside Aberdulais
a bank of light
sandy-clay alluvium
or glacial till
scattered throughout with
many pot-rounded pebbles

& in the cages were
fox & other mammals
dull-eyed & quiver-breathed
African eagle mid-black
with ferocious red beak
ruminating over carrion wreckage
making short heavy flights
from bar to bar
within the narrow confines of the cage
& a rowing Alsatian guard dog,
chained up

"Subsidence was pulsatory, however,"
heaving up & down like
an ancient animal in sleep

a wrinkled hide rippling
a touch of volcanics, rolling
smoke & dust clouds,
breccias & acid plutonic intrusions,
tuffs & ashes & lava flows
now an outwash of debris in intense rainfall
the storms tearing the rocks apart
washing the debris over arid plains
quartz fragments driven seaward
to mingle with mudswarm
settling in the foredeep
turbid slumping in the lower sediments
now uplift & coal peat bed composites
under tangle of giant fern
again invaded by muddy seas
then calcium carbonate deposition
in another clear, calm, shallow sea
Subsidence was pulsatory
the Neath Valley Disturbance
soup-plate crack settling
grinding edge
of the Hercynian orogeny
metamorphosis of deposits
formation of the fine anthracites
of the Vale of Neath

Glory of the morning
I recite the name of Tiw
Name
      a thing
& you gain a measure
of power
      & then there is
naming the Devil
which sends him away
            defence
      interpolation
interstice   insight   love
It is by naming
that we handle each other
or castigating   with malice

Beyond the conflict lies
wisdom?   But this
precipitational doubt
these quirks &
despairing heaves
of the unstable compound
& each time gulfs open
that you never knew were there
& each time
the pain of reaching
seems to be more

Two eyes of the Ox,
the Lair of the Greyhound Bitch,
ravens flowing against the wind,
bonking their melancholy
corvine bark
A bronze saw set with
jewelled teeth
stone hammers
                    in the hand of man
his half-roasted meals
                    of flesh
The Cross
            of Gwallter, a half-roofed
stone hutment on the highest point,
set where a man could
see South, & Sun, & be
sheltered.   Limestone
bone-structure, loosely
sketched in turf,
frizzed-out thorn clamped
close   embracing
the rock   in obeisance
to the winds' will of years,
waters percolating,
dissolving away
to dank echoing caverns
below.

A conspiracy to draw
the great white worm
from the depths of the earth.

CARREG BICA.   Massive.   Myriad
initials
carved on the sandstone forefinger
threatening the sky
drawing from the earth source.
A man asks me, "What is
the meaning of this stone?"
"It's a beacon
for flying saucers in the sky,"
I reply   helplessly

St Valentine's Day . . .

. . . utter clarity
pressure rising
the land afloat
on love messages
six white wavelets
athwart the sky
thrilling tight vee
of six white birds
rowing strongly
from horizon to horizon
sun reflecting bright
from pale underwing
a rough grit conglomerate
sparkling with quartz pebbles
set into the matrix
barn owl flaps
over the burnt conifers
denizen of the cartroom
at Glan yr Afon
stone gothic folly
whose vibrations
prick Mena's skin
she had said to me
in the New Inn
amid the rattling crash
of stentorian conversation
Dai roaring over his pint
his face aglow
today brings his gun
& hounds & terriers
to the burrows
to hunt fox
as I drift down to the river
to pick up
water-rolled & bruised
orange shale, & long arm
of storm-wrenched damp ash
to be brought back & dried

small birds bobbing
  through bare branches of alder
   insoucient haze
drapes down over the South-Western basin
    while aimless stratus casts
  sharp blue shadows
   onto the hills
the fire-tower conning
   blindly, uselessly

The Diary of Palug's Cat

Walking
the hill
first I knew
spiny
evisceral
press roll
of tarry black wings
2 excited ravens
crowding by
at vast speed
dicing with each other
like a couple of fighter pilots
low level attack flying
creaking between the trees
then up in a loop
not half-a-wingbeat between 'em
to engineer a breathless somersault
at the height of their climb
then down again
in a vertical dive
to collision & disaster
missed by an inch
up & down over the
valley in
waves till gone
from sight

I have an idea
certain compartments in my head
are very firmly
                locked
                        shut

    WHAT THE HELL
WENT WRONG WITH MY MARRIAGE?

Others, equally,
are bolted
wide open

the sense of freedom
buzzards swirling.   The blue sky
beckoning.   The powder-yellow
catkin haze.   Damp lambs
struggling alive
on the close, soaked turf

Glyn Neath.   Everyone
buying flowers for Easter.   Feast
of the Dead.   Burning
of the last sacrifice
of the dark year.
"She won't be back."
The clod turns.
the worm squirms.
Following the dictates
of my unreason –
let it be said
this epitaph
is sheer nonsense, a joke
but one that for years
has brilliantly fulfilled its function
     as a flypaper
for every conceivable
projection that has
buzzed in my mind.
Sometimes a diagnosis
as between creativity & tomfoolery
is difficult to make
as it happens again & again
that the 2 are confused.   The
curly pubic hairs of a virgin
are converted into a fine powder
upon which
     the fancy
       of the folk
         delights to linger.

Rubric.   A tomb must be dug
for the Dragon & the Woman.
Trenching to great depth
in yielding damp soil
filling same full
of weedy turves
slamming cowshit on top
spade suck toil lift
turn batter cleave enveloping
the green seed potato with its
fragile easily broken sprouts
the gulls somehow distant &
uncompromisingly handsome
bending a wing
with muted grace
over the slough
of turned ground

Cylinder Fragments of the Twentieth Century

2 goldcrests, a few feet away,
excitedly hopping like mad
intimately round the scraggly
old hawthorn branch, picking
delicately at invisible
microscopic things, so close,
so intent were they, such a
comprehensive little unit of
togetherness, 2 tiny goldcrests
with their tiny shrill
raindrop voices, flicking & zapping
delicately through complex bristly
thorny outgrowths without stopping
in their flitting movement

Byron
scythed his moto up the slurry track
& told me the car was waiting by the gate.
I got in the back seat beside Jan,
Val & Chris in the front, Rubin
                      parked amidships
we all went to the red lion   LLEW COCH
& supped Feeling Foul, & I rapped with my favourite
her long dark hair flashing a redgold strand
   Less obsessed, I should have pondered more
on the ley of Scots pine pointing down the valley
to Kilvey & Gower; the list of real ales in the bar;
the squat little Cynog church crouched to the rain
at a thousand feet, overlooking 100 square miles
of crinkled land surface, veiled in eternal rains.
Instead, I noticed her bitten-down nails, & loved her again,
so beat, clay-stained, trailing off behind Byron on pillion
in thin skirt on wet bike.

The Book of Brychan

Resolving
        to set the
                Brychan monolith

                    U
                    P
                    R
                    I
                    G
                    H
                    T

I have made a heap
             of discovered things

4th/5th century A.D. –
           famine, plague & pestilence
           affect proto-Brecknock

Marchella, daughter to Tewdrig of Garth Madryn
to Ireland, with 300 retainers, to seek a husband

2/3rds of her force
            perish of the cold
                  on the way over

Marchella brings back as consort
Amlach, son of Coronach, a king of Ireland

of the union
           of Marchella & Amlach
                  is born BRYCHAN
eponymous founder of a dynasty
           that lasts 500 years, half a millennium!
'It takes not sloth
           to found a dynasty'

The kingdom of Brycheiniog survives
        an almost Egyptian length of non-history time
for there is no direct history of this time
        a legion of legends
        a few inscribed stones

At an early age, Brychan was sent into fosterage with the king of
neighbouring Powys, as was the custom of those times; & the
young prince came under the tutelage of the soothsayer
Driccan, ' . . . who, although then blind, saw a vision on the
riverbank, at the confluence of the Honddu with the Usk, of a
wild boar; & in the water behind the boar there was a stag, &
under the stag swam a fish. A beech tree grew on the riverbank,
& in the tree bees had made a honeycomb . . .'

the vision   foretelling, presumably,
                      that the fruits of the land
                      would be under Brychan's governaunce

Later, Brychan, by persistent legend, has some twentyfour
daughters & sixteen sons, both in & out of marriage, numbers
varying in different manuscripts

Many of these daughters & sons became early Christian saints,
founding in the 5th century A.D. many llanau or monastic
settlements which are often strategically placed for the defence
of the borders of Brycheiniog

Stones were set up by the wayside
        in the Roman fashion
& specifically on the military road network
        that stayed in use until medieval times
certainly Llia, the feminine lozenge,
        wide-hipped, ponderous, earth-wise
        is more of an enigma
than the redbrown, fiery, upright
        pillar of Dervacus, son of Justus
        bedded in the causeway, Sarn Helen
1500 years a vibrant node
        accumulating wind & water power
        sun power, earth power
        resistance slowing down the sphere

dug up by
> modern archaeologists who affirmed
> a large square cistvaen
> but no human remains
> in the acid humus

The Celtic Church cut off from Rome 150 years
on the Western fringes of the dissociating empire
the seas controlled by barbarians & pirates
yet hermetic ideas filtered up from the Med
the roadside stones paralleled
>> in North Africa
the early Christianity a patina
> warped & woofed upon
> the more ancient palimpsest of druidism

A Further Canto for Brychan

... he   early   having had issue
      Cynog
out of wedlock
      from Benadlinet
a princess of the
House of Powys
wherein he was fostered

... a hot lord was he and unlettered
      that knew to correct his own faults

... but Brychan stored grain against famine
& rode the federation territories
    kept peace on the frontiers
    'easy to start a war, less
    easy to finish one'
– brought calm in vine climate
      breasthills of the kingdom

... rents & forfeitures were abolished
'you can't rook people who have so little'
– gained their co-operation instead

& consulted the wise women of the parishes
    those splendid pictesses, Cymry, co-proprietors,
speckled folk of stones & trackways
    herb women, washers at the ford

the old laws memorized, coded in dry doggerel
the Christian precepts gradually absorbed & adapted
an overlay grafted onto custom & usage
    legend & season-stone

each princeling or chieftain
    leading his kindred
    to baptism
– druids sons to monasteries
    - daughters to nunneries

even

   as poets

       we must err

& stay in touch

   with the earthbound

& suffer our own

        possessiveness

we are not angels

    though of angelic wing

(& stolen light)

clinging to

     the damaged sphere

stink of fuel oil from the ocean

that is the familiar bitter note

I cannot ignore sitting out

in the closed-in valley where

curlews cry, my paradise-orchard

the green foaming masses

making May mighty

        where winter had been for so long

Cities of ant barrows

      populating strategic ground

the wriggling of

      trees branches into the sky

the earth's

      coiled ball of energies

the orange shale pavement

      an interstitial in the Grit series

      I consult the leaning man

      at the crossroads, holed

      top & bottom   perhaps

      a very old railway sleeper

            definitely

      a sleeper

the capsule upended in the earth

the eternal poem in motion through time

attuned to the curve of the zodiac

In the Country

The autumn doesn't come to hilly South Wales in tapestries of
gorgeous colour, it comes in a quiet, muted way; first, the
birches turn a few leaves pale yellow, then perhaps you see one
or two of them have suddenly dropped all their leaves, & just a
few withered ones remain. The pale ash, last to come, first to go,
drops after the first firm frosts. The hawthorn flashes briefly
through a sequence, dropping a coppery carpet. The alder sheds
its leaves, still more green than brown, & the oaks let go
reluctantly, many keeping a full canopy of leaves throughout the
winter that blazes orange against deep blue winter skies. Down
in the vale if you're lucky you'll see the vivid hues of chestnut,
or the flaming of a few rare beeches. No, it's not the autumn
that's colourfully impressive here, full of quiet magic though it
is; it's the winter when this type of country really shows its
variety of texture. Then lichens on rocks glow like spray-blown
tube station graffiti, silver-white galaxies explode on starmap
slabs; bright green mosses & orangey asphodel skeletons stick
up out of the mires of the rough grazing, that sometimes reflect
brilliant oily cobalt, sending up a stench of algaic, gaseous
intensity when stepped in; the grass tufts going suddenly
coppery-blonde in the autumn, turning into brilliant, bleached
straw through the late winter.

This is Wales; not the tourist Wales of over-popular Snowdonia
or Gower, but the North-Western rim of the coalfield, a funny,
nooky, complicated tossup of a landscape, already geologically
tumbled, into which man has poured to wrest the mineral
wealth, as it were haphazard from the rocks; his holes & caverns
& wastepiles & derelict buildings & shantywork are everywhere.
One of Europe's biggest strip mines, Maes Gwyn Cap, eating its
way into the North Crop. The Penderyn quarry carving away at
the limestone pushed up by the Neath Valley Fault. Other
numerous open-cast sites smoothed over by the efforts of the
environmentally conscious 20th century. Forest claiming up to
2/3rds of the whole Fforest Fawr–Neath Valley region; the
Commission owning 11% of Wales. But it's still *country*, or more
correctly *space*. The feeling of openness overhead & around
oneself, room to think, time in which to think it. I never had
time to really think in the city.

The green woodpecker bounces over furze & stunted oak, & a mist lies like a becalmed whale in the Cwm; & one feels a tenacious attachment to this wet, intractable, near-naked bit of barrenness, with its opencast site wounds, untidy gashes of clear-cut timber in blanket forestry, urban valley sprawl. Ribbon city in the country, grimy terraces & eternal gossipy corner shops with buses wheeling by in blue fumes & a harsh engine roar... yet step up a small steep tarmac road or a rutted lane & you step onto a hillside where a ewe stares at you & stamps her foot in irritation, before turning away with her lamb & joining a little group that will run off in a disciplined, dodging manner among the red-gold brake & steely heather, a stream will purl down the hillside, a kestrel hang on the crest of the hill...

As I write in this place, I can feel the absoluteness of the quiet, flowing around my body, flowing through my consciousness...& the deeper, slower motions & archetypes of the psyche become revealed. I become more tuned in to the dreams in my head, the nature of the past, & of the present moment; & to speculate on the future. The absolute silence of the place I'm in sharpens the play of possibilities that is the constant factor when I'm writing...

I remember during the first year, feeling adrift in all that self-created free time; how could it possibly be filled?

Then there were, and are, those days upon days when the conditions of dripping welsh hill mist virtually confined one to the house, without t.v. & only a scratchy radio ear to the outside world.

But when the good days came along, the miracle started right there on the doorstep, with several types of ferns & lichens as well as mosses in the garden wall... striking dark blue flowers of brooklime in the streamy gutter just outside; the scent of wild honeysuckle tantalising as one walked up the narrow tarmac road; flowers, birds, trees, frogs, lizards, toads, newts, wasps, midges; bloodthirsty horseflies that followed one around on summer days magnetized by sweating human skin, drawn as if by radar to the underwrist, to the hollow of the throat... the dragonflies that enchanted with dazzling, clicking flight, fritillaries crowding on dame's violet in early June, the brown hoverflies clustered on the ivy flowers in St Luke's Little Summer in mid-October... to the suburban-citybred consciousness, this was all brand new territory, new naming, new knowledge. The beginning of the understanding of the natural miracle.

It's really difficult to explain wanting to be a writer, let alone a poet, in the late 20th century, especially when it's coupled up to the usual material expectations of either stardom or failure, with no medium ground allowed inbetween, where the writing becomes a natural expression & extension of your existence.. where you're actually at.

I was up the slope, with the little ruin on my right, when I met William Davies & we must have talked for nearly an hour – mainly of the cairns I had been trying to locate in the forestry, but also of drystonewalling – walls built almost vertically up mountainsides – examples of good stonewalling and building – the later Pen Fathor house "fantastic good"; the lime kilns that had such good coigns; boundary heaps and the "Seven Foot Stone"; the Old Red Sandstone menhir at Battle; Maen Llia, Maen Madoc; "beating the bounds". We stood there in the sun and frost on wet pasture with yellowy dried wispy tussocks; & I noted the bashed & blackened thumbnail, the blunt round fingers like bananas; the butt he drew at one point from a vest pocket, rolled in his mouth for a few sentences, lit it, took one puff, blew out the smoke immediately, the butt went out, to be restored to his pocket again; a blunt, quiet stocky man with thick pebble glasses & an ancient postman's jacket, his old dog rushing off & then reporting back again at regular 5 minute intervals.

The Slim Book

the

shades of

autumn surging

& showering

the pale flush

of leaf-death, the

acorn

bombardment with

every gentle breeze

a

dream of a

saint's grave

shaped like

a boat

dumb &

still

just felt like

crying somehow

shaking a tree

leaves clatter down

snow –

grains

    & collies

run their muzzles

along the surface

with every appearance

of delight

      further down

the valley

is so vulgar

as to have

no snow

    this area

which stays nameless & remote

    blanket

afforested & distant

the low sun

reveals every grassblade

soft patchwork of fields

    hill by hill

leading to the mountains

heartburst of tenderness at this

50,000 nuclear warheads

    poised

to rub it all to waste

RORI: A Book of the Boundaries

DIS

    the old underworld

    the white underworld

Vaynor

      the last pagan refuge

in these saint-dotted hills of Brychan

         sanded   abraded

peneplains &   occasional summits

           serrated escarpments

limestone knives like teeth

set upright in the turf

narrow stream

flows

under the Old Church

floating sprays of celeriac green

creamy succubi

of the hemlock umbrella

constant shift

from the frame

of the real

into an infinite,

mythic dissolve

    no boundaries to the universe

   no boundaries to time

  no boundaries to sensation

no boundaries to message

    that is the terror & the beauty

    the measure blends back to us

    The Beautiful Daughters of Vaynor

"transformed into rivers & streams", guiding

the traveller in mist & fog & tempest

    dippers' nest in the lace curtains

take shapes from nature

omens in the flight of birds

entrails of sacrifices

    firecracked

shoulderblade of a ram

labyrinthine readings of THE WORD

glyph   language

of fossil limestone

    the WORD begins

sky so blue   so clear

a silver dollar   & then swept by

bright white fierce sharp hail

                salty minerals slide

between freezing facets

Vaynor, "Place of the Boundaries"

the star map imprinted in his head

"to whence thou shalt return"

Indian handpumped harmonium

gypsey fair on a windy hill

panting diesel generators

thrumming artillery of machinery

He rides the Sunboat of Millions of Years

the celestial Barge of Aten

towed by 8 Oxen of the Sun

fox triple tongue in the wildwood

Praise Poem to Neith

Within the precinct of your beneficence,
O Neith, healer & strengthener, I come to
                sing your praises
shades of blue in your silvered blackness
rolling by mossdark boulder shore

I am absorbed in the dream of you,
sunpath goddess, sky-stretched,
guardian goddess of day.   Thy
white girdle, O Neith, of high-
drawn water   spring source
flowing
        ledge by ledge
                        crook by garn
from sunrise to sunset
        from spring to sea
                sky goddess Neith
                        carry me
into womb of being

Green thine eyes, flecked with rainbow,
scudding fringe of sweetness surrounds you
                        oxbow curve
elevates me on high, renewed
        day by day by you
shelf by shelf, plane by plane, I am your layers,
sun & star-burned conglomerate delta
I am fulfilled in your generous embrace,
lady of daytime light, hope, fruit
I am exulted in your presence,
raising my hands in salutation on
                        kingfisher reach;
I am shy sliver moon reflecting
scarce one iota of your brilliance

river's deep tabor
announces your presence
falcon rush of
majestic immanence
wild white eye of the sky
I bow down in humility, & bathe
in your radiance

O Neith, I drink your nectar
bees in a noisy cloud
issue from your hair
I dissolve into your bosom
of inspiration & delight.

The King's Royal Moor

The long   :   field

the red   :   marsh

the king's   :   waen

the king's   :   common

made a gift of it   :   to his commoners

the king's royal common   :   Hirwaen

& that king's wine   :   was mead

Urban ribbon
stretching
from Nantgarw stack
blowing white tumbling clouds

right to here
where Borrow strides
towards Merthyr's hells

a million miles
these stout boots
falling apart

eventually
only a
slab of
indestructible sole
will be left

a slab of my soul

From Hirwaen along the
old trunk road to the Don cafe

highrise blocks
dumped here on this sublime col

the king's   royal   moor,
                              the
Tower Washery
                  cones & lakes
of black spill

the mega-opencast
operation

mountains
made by God,
remade by man

coughing machinery
travelling in dustclouds

Three tattered thorns
                    reveal
subsistence farming before
the black klondike

a kind of prosperity
in spells of better climate

the Cistercian monks
at their most optimistic

the king's
            royal
                    mead
today poor, mean, acid land

great gastank
on the treeless moorline
at 300 metres

grey concrete-clad
mushroom uprising
from its caul

Places
most people only want to leave

flight from
restless dogbarking estates

perfunctory exercises in
new light industry

sheep grazing under
glaring fluoros

police & picket line violence
during the coal strike

bleary old bum scores VP
from the halal grocers

smudgy youth offers
a gram of white powder

a beguiling scent of gorse
from a sunny pocket

a limousine ride to the
wrecker's yard, crusher
in fast forward gear

& the royal mead
                    a drink fit for a king

the royal meadow
                    now this
irregular warren
crazed through fault-ridden
sheared & split rock layers
                    with hasty remodelling

deserts of black & grey

fast growing
                    willowtree roundabout
swallows night drivers

& bandits hid in the groves & canyons
crouched in blackened heather moor

ambushed coal trains
in well-rehearsed hordes

teevee cameras at the crossroads
lenses pointed right down
into our white upraised faces
in the cab of the truck

prickly galvanised neurones dance

an afternoon goes by in a whiff of diesel

bone powder slowly dissipating

sea breeze front
pushes coking plant
pollution inland
locked under the inversion

retailored tips,
firehazard carpets

Baglan Mountain
burned 3 days
a chaos of exploding, tossing flames
creeping against the windstream
individual trees
torching up like napalm

Central Europe
gathers thunder to itself

remembrance of war, of prison camp,
                                    body jelly

                    the sky   could be so blue
til split by Phantom or
        B52 giant spider
flying low upvalley, wingtips
almost touching the valley's sides

skimming double lines of pylons
jumping to the Black Alps of Banwen

mineworkings
straddle the Roman Road
charcoal hearth
shudders under
spoil-buried cars of
insurance ripoffs
giant tipper shaking
Bronze Age buckle

Pedol Haern stirs in
layered millennial sleep
newforged iron horseshoe in hand
lunar crescent moving ever outward
drawing the veil of illusion

Prisoners   in, on or about the world
                    in, on, or about the excitable body
wind onrushing the ideas that leave no trace
                    blossom thin in a drought land

sex chatter   on pulsing field nets
     refractive index   shading through meaning
                      a thousand times a second

     NO   fixed point
     NO   frozen magma
     NO   virgin in the stone arms of the god

   instead
a blackened cadaver stutters
          from one prohibition to the next
                neck in knots
            wobbling pizzle
          spraycanning graffiti under the stars

          monsters of our making
          wither at the boundary

          a teardrop of reality
          honeytanks of scam

Angel Busted
(For Chris Jenkins)

Mountains, moors, crags & quarryings,
rail inclines to the sky & beyond
       estates on rolling hillspurs

unloved, tattered streets
torn posters ripping off
boarded shopfronts,
pale windy sunshine
flaring across silver rooves
       to dunes & seas & drowned cities

privet shivers in a thrash of wind
leaves falling, words twisting
fierce twigs from the sun
caught in his sox
angel fries in cold steel

a sudden phalanx of paranoid swords
strident star sirens of interference
aluminium boneheads bleached of thought

hired guns, alloymen, disposal experts
crystal men & dropmen, bagmen & dead bodies
tarnished warriors clanking their lasers masers
       particle beam accelerators
cryptic fundamentalist mullahs arousing
       from cold minarets

mirrorbright caffeine raps an easy smile
fierce twigs from the sun caught in his sox
angel arrest rivets the coaltown
angel fries in cold steel

privet shivers in a thrash of wind
hired guns, alloymen, disposal experts
crystalmen & dropmen, bagmen & dead bodies
posters ripping off rotted shopfronts

torn, unloved, tattered streets
estates on rolling hillspurs
strident star sirens of interference
angel arrest rivets the coaltown
angel fries in cold steel
angel fries in cold steel

Maytime

(for Barry MacSweeney)

with sexy delight
      songthrush celebrates
riff after riff
      glories of May

      ragged as
      walkway busker's piping
           – pigeon's
      tailfeathers

ancient trees   modern noise
      agitation acute
planet endures

just above stalling
         red kite
creeps over turf
         my scavenger ego
shadowed by buzzards

skeletons in cupboards
    infinite intangibles
    act of writing shakes
      wobbly chair

build sound dome all day
    insect instruments   leaf whisper
a single combustion
    destroys in an instant

    smooth lenticulars
    brow of an angel
    over charred grass

    tilt of a double axe
    over a screaming stone
    the dominion of man

each wind rocks
    wobbly chair

each tectonic wave
        shakes the skull
                whipped by
                spider silk

          death of a brother

    windblown pipit
    takes your soul
    out over rushes

a shiver up my spine
your crab cancer
        implacable smile

Shootout on Slate Street

Clean kitchen surfaces   2 slabs of black slate
finish the job   with a swipe   hide or cover
all food
              FINALLY
                          reach for the
resealed superlager under my chair
                                    funny,
                            the seal is off
but I pour   & drink   pour again   as I
turn the can over something bumps   yes
              there's a BODY in there
                          mouse
                          lager

So what to do now?   Volunteering myself
in the cause of disinterested research
              I swig again

                    O SPIRIT
of frisky, amusing mouse, pesky thief a shade
forever scratching in corners   I had sworn
NOT to kill you, following my initial rage
at finding turds in my soup   nibbled carrots
chewed tomatoes   your impudent raids
swaggering on Slate Street, twirling
              6 shooter mustache whiskers -
              - mice toes scampering -

I could have left the top off the milk & you would
have dived in & drowned: but I didn't -   So now
what have you done?

O noble mouse,
blithe & bibulous, of bright eye, huge
lucent ears & long tail   a fast getaway
in a customized Mustang, a Mercedes 280SL, an
old Cortina dragging its sump

this tin of alcohol was your downfall: o scatterbrain,
deluded, silky mouse   my habit killed you
dead as duck soup
                        I imbibe your spirit
in recognition of my immutable fate, tiny beast so unafraid
when I shone my Coleman lamp upon you in the black
November night of your perky triumph
                            now you are dead,
head down in a can of lager.   Mouse,
with this last gulp I take you aboard my raft:
you can travel with me on the
                            lager trail forever

Hermits

1000 yards of mud
in any direction

      & some cows

      & this house

is all there is

a sweaty   greasy   heaving sky

      is all there is
        all there is

of rain
      100 inches
         the fields

puckled & poached   the flock
blackened   humped   saturated

      is all there is

HEAR
    the old ram's
    guttural bass roar
    dewy fleeces pounding
    in perverse mists

      peregrine's
      frenzied yakking
      - someone's
      rusty wheelbarrow

WRITE
      a hermit poem   write
      a poem about a hermit   he
      lives on an island   a path runs
      round the island   there is a
      volcano in the middle
          It is the self

                        two lizards
                  entangled in a drainpipe
                        so much in love

stop for a time
stop for a rhyme
              river flow
Is endless

                      the broken rucksack
                a winebox too far

    mass: a
          dark suitcase
    lost in the void

                against wetblack, frowning
                mountain   white butterfly
                dances in sunlight

          on this ancient crab,
          leafless, sun-facing
          a single, yellow fruit

PREVIOUS PUBLICATIONS

GRAHAM HARTILL

Poems taken from *Cennau's Bell* (The Collective Press, 2005), *A Winged Head* (Parthian Books, 2007), and *Chroma* (Boiled String Chapbooks, Hafan Press, 2014)

PHIL MAILLARD

Some of Phil Maillard's poems in *Slipping the Leash* appeared in two of his books: *Coming Up From Silence* (Canna, 1999), and *Sweet Dust and Growling Lambs* (Shearsman, 2008).

They also appeared in the following books and magazines: *Arcade, Beneath The Underground, Cabaret 246, ctrl+alt+del, Fire, Frames, Global Tapestry Journal, Holy Wells: Wales*, by Phil Cope (Seren, 2008), *Poetry Wales, Scintilla*, and *The English Path*, by Kim Taplin (Perry Green Press, 2nd Ed'n., 2000).

CHRIS TORRANCE

Selected from the following books:

Acrospirical Meanderings in a Tongue of the Time
   Albion Village, London, 1973.
The Magic Door. Book One
   Albion Village, London, 1975.
Citrinas
   The Magic Door Book 2. Albion Village, London, 1977.
The Diary of Palug's Cat
   The Magic Door Book 3. Galloping Dog, Newcastle, 1980.
Cylinder Fragments of the Twentieth Century
   Cwm Nedd, Neath Abbey, 1982.
The Book of Brychan
   The Magic Door Book 4. Galloping Dog, Newcastle, 1982.
The Slim Book/Wet Pulp
   The Magic Door Book 5. Stone Lantern, Swansea, 1986.
The Tempers of Hazard (with Thomas A. Clark and Barry
   MacSweeney) Paladin, London 1993

Southerly Vector/The Book of Heat
Further books of The Magic Door. (Cwm Nedd, Neath Abbey,
1996)

Wobbly Chair
Canna, Cardiff, 2003.

Hermits
(with Barry Edgar Pilcher and Bill Wyatt). Canna, Cardiff,
2003)

Rori: A Book of the Boundaries
(text and CD, with Chris Vine). Heat Poets, 2011.

THE AUTHORS

Graham Hartill: as a teenager Graham became fascinated by avant-garde music and theatre and staged a few chaotic performances. He moved to Wales and went on to study in the USA. On his return in 1980 he met Chris Torrance and Phil Maillard and became a mainstay of the burgeoning poetry scene in Cardiff. Graham taught in China and in the early nineties was invited to take up a residency in Scotland where he was involved in the Open World Poetics movement. He is now a writer-in-residence at HMP Parc, facilitates in the field of writing in health and social care and in 2013 became the first writer-in-residence at Swansea College of Medicine. He lives in the Black Mountains with his family.

Phil Maillard was born in 1948 in South London. He completed a carpentry apprenticeship with the old Greater London Council in the early 1970's. He moved to South Wales in 1975, and now lives in the Cardiff area. Allen Fisher and John Freeman published his first books, in the mid-70's. In the early 1980's he ran creative writing groups for the Welsh Academi (now Literature Wales) and the University of Wales, and commenced some small press and community publishing. For twenty years he worked for the NHS as a Speech and Language Therapist, specialising in progressive neurological conditions. Since retiring in 2008, he has worked with people with Alzheimer's Disease, and has also spent increasing amounts of time in Spain. Maillard was much influenced in his writing by an early connection (1967 onwards) with Chris Torrance. He is married to nature photographer Val Maillard.

Chris Torrance was born in Edinburgh, Scotland, in 1941. In the late 1940's his parents took him down to Surrey. He started work as a legal executive in 1957, but by 1965 he had given up the law and begun work as a Parks Department labourer, with the intention of taking writing seriously, and especially poetry, which was inspired by the experience of being in the open air. He helped edit the magazine ORIGINS DIVERSIONS, and his work began to appear in various little mags and anthologies. By 1970 he was living in a rural area of South Wales, just north of the coalfield, where he began his multi-volume series, THE MAGIC DOOR. From 1976 - 2001 Torrance ran an evening class - ADVENTURES IN CREATIVE WRITING - for U.C. Cardiff, from which emerged the group and magazine CABARET 246. Since the mid 1980's, with Chris Vine working as HEATPOETS, he has created a series of CD's of poetry and music. A large collection - PATH - is awaiting publication.